We <u>ARE</u> Americans

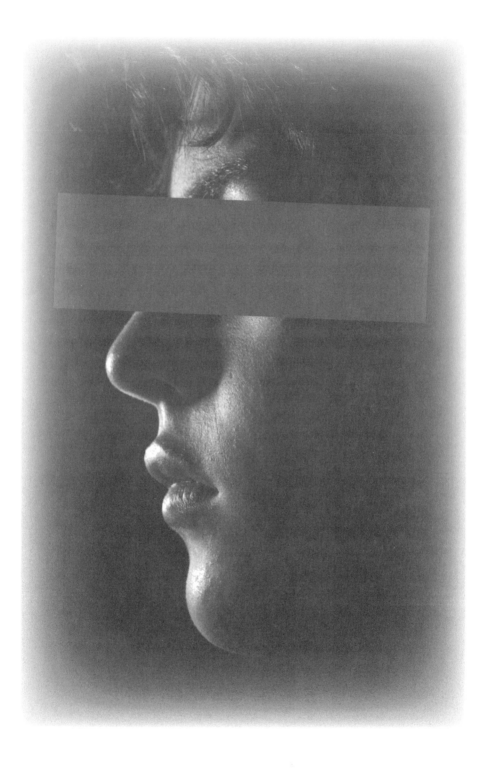

We <u>ARE</u> Americans

Undocumented Students Pursuing the American Dream

WILLIAM PEREZ

Foreword by DANIEL SOLORZANO

STERLING, VIRGINIA

COPYRIGHT © 2009
BY STYLUS PUBLISHING, LLC.

Published by Stylus Publishing, LLC
22883 Quicksilver Drive
Sterling, Virginia 20166-2102

Library of Congress Cataloging-in-Publication-Data
Perez, William, 1974-
   We are Americans : Undocumented students pursuing the American dream / William Perez ; foreword by Daniel Solorzano.—1st ed.
      p. cm.
   Includes bibliographical references and index.
   ISBN 978-1-57922-375-5 (cloth : alk. paper)
   ISBN 978-1-57922-376-2 (pbk. : alk. paper)
      1. Educational equalization—United States—Case studies.   2. Discrimination in education—United States—Case studies.   3. Illegal aliens—Education—United States—Case studies.   4. Illegal aliens—United States—Anecdotes.   5. United States—Emigration and immigration.   I. Title.
LC213.2.P46   2009
371 826'910973—dc22   2009026206

13-digit ISBN: 978-1-57922-375-5 (cloth)
13-digit ISBN: 978-1-57922-376-2 (paper)

Printed in the United States of America

All first editions printed on acid free paper that meets the American National Standards Institute Z39-48 Standard.

Bulk Purchases

Quantity discounts are available for use in workshops and for staff development.
Call 1-800-232-0223

First Edition, 2009

10   9   8   7   6   5   4

*This book is dedicated
to all undocumented students
pursuing the American dream.*

CONTENTS

PART FIVE
Formerly Undocumented College Graduates

FOREWORD

IN late March of 2006, thousands of high school students across the country walked out in support of better-quality schools in Latina/o communities and for the rights of undocumented students at all levels of the education pipeline. On May 1, 2006, well over a million people throughout the United States demonstrated for the rights of undocumented people and against proposed federal legislation titled the *Border Protection, Antiterrorism, and Illegal Immigration Control Act* (H.R. 4437). This proposed law would have mandated a felony charge against any undocumented person found to be residing in the United States, and it barred undocumented residents from ever gaining legal status in the United States. Although the demonstrations were seen as important milestones in the historical struggle for immigrant rights, they are part of a larger history of struggle for human rights in the United States, and indeed around the world. This period also became a significant catalyst for an important body of research on the undocumented community generally and undocumented students in particular. Professor William Perez has become an intellectual leader in this critical area of research; in the spring of 2006 he began the project from which the 20 interviews for his book *We ARE Americans* are drawn.

Although quantifying the number of undocumented Latina/o immigrants residing in the United States remains a challenge, current estimates provide a sense of their significance within the U.S. population. The U.S. Census Bureau (2004) estimates that in 2004 there were 34 million foreign-born residents in the United States. Of these 34 million people, almost 53 percent were Latina/o. In the same year, just over 9 million foreign-born residents lived in California, of whom 55 percent were Latina/o. The U.S. Census does not report the legal status of foreign-born immigrants, but in a recent report the *Pew Hispanic Center* estimates that around 12 million undocumented people live in the United States (Passel, 2006). When we look at the Latina/o educational pipeline, we see enormous leaks at high school graduation, baccalaureate completion, and graduate and professional school degrees (Perez Huber, Huidor, Malagon, & Solorzano, 2006; Yosso & Solorzano, 2006). When we examine Latina/o non-citizens, the numbers are even worse (Guarneros, Bendezu, Perez Huber, Velez, & Solorzano, 2009; Perez Huber, Malagon, & Solorzano, 2009).

Whether in legislation, public policy, or the media, utilizing a language of exclusion and charges of economic and social cost are key constructs in framing the Latina/o immigration issue. The terms *illegal alien, illegal immigrant, illegals, undocumented workers, undocumented immigrants, guest workers, temporary workers, braceros, and "wetbacks"* have been used throughout U.S. history to refer to Latina/o immigrants crossing the border and residing in the United States. However, no matter how the issue is framed, one thing seems to hold constant: The framing of the debate around "immigration reform" has focused primarily on immigrants themselves, void of any significant discussions about the forces or structures that create the international migration of people. From a historical and economic standpoint, immigration reform has stratified Latina/o immigrants in a way that encouraged their incorporation into the U.S. labor market economy while denying them full membership into U.S. society. The exclusionary nature of immigration reform has been its most characteristic feature since the signing of the Treaty of Guadalupe Hidalgo in 1848 (Perez Huber, Benavides, Malagon, Velez, & Solorzano, 2008; Velez, Perez Huber, Benavides, de la Luz, & Solorzano, 2008). However, there is a growing body of research that reframes immigration and immigrant issues and focuses on the vast array of social and cultural wealth these communities bring to the world generally and to the United States in particular (Abrego, 2006; Gonzales, 2007, 2008, 2009; Olivérez, 2007; Perez, Espinoza, Ramos, Coronado, & Cortes, 2009; Perez Huber et al., 2008; Perez Huber & Malagon, 2007; Rangel, 2001; UCLA Center for Labor Research and Education, 2008; Velez et al., 2008, Yosso, 2005, 2006). Dr. Perez's book, *We ARE Americans*, is an essential part of that research.

We ARE Americans begins by placing undocumented people at the center of the story and in a much-needed historical and contemporary context. Professor Perez provides the evidence to challenge the notion that undocumented people are a drain on social services and makes the argument that they have contributed, and continue to contribute, significantly to our nation's economic and social well-being. Starting with Penelope, a highly motivated and tenacious high school senior and ending with Nicole, a newly minted Ph.D., Professor Perez has crafted 20 compelling portraits of resilience and survival in a social and educational world that continuously places barriers in the paths of these gifted and talented scholars.

Over a century ago, John Dewey (1900) pushed us to pursue the anti-elitist position that "What the best and brightest parent wants for his [her] *own* child, that must the community want for *all* its children" (p. 3) (emphasis mine). I concur with Dewey and emphasize that *all* includes undocumented students. Professor Perez's research provides persuasive evidence that the talent we lose when we exclude undocumented students is a devastating loss to the United States and to our values of "equal justice under law" and "equal educational opportunity."

Daniel G. Solorzano
Professor of Social Science & Comparative Education
Graduate School of Education & Information Studies
University of California, Los Angeles

References

Abrego, L. (2006). 'I can't go to college because I don't have papers': Incorporation patterns of Latino undocumented youth. *Latino Studies Journal, 4,* 212–231.

Dewey, J. (1900). *The school and society.* Chicago: The University of Chicago Press.

Gonzales, R. (2007). Wasted talent and broken dreams: The lost potential of undocumented students. *Immigration Policy in Focus,* 5(13). Washington, DC: Immigration Policy Service.

Gonzalez, R. (2008). Left out, but not shut down: Political activism and the undocumented student movement. *Northwestern Journal of Law and Social Policy*, 3, 219–239.

Gonzalez, R. (2009). *Young lives on hold: The college dreams of undocumented students*. New York: College Board.

Guarneros, N., Bendezu, C., Perez Huber, L., Velez, V., & Solorzano, D. (May 2009). Still dreaming: Legislation and legal decisions affecting undocumented AB 540 students. *Latino Policy & Issues Brief No. 23*, UCLA Chicano Studies Research Center.

Lackoff, G., & Ferguson, S. (May 2006). *The framing of immigration*. Unpublished report. Berkeley, CA: Rockridge Institute.

Olivérez, P. (2007). A perilous path: Undocumented immigrant students and the college pipeline. *Metropolitan Universities Journal*, 18, 87–101.

Passel, J. (2006). *The size and characteristics of the unauthorized migrant population in the U.S.: Estimates based on the March 2005 current population survey*. Research Report. Washington, DC: Pew Hispanic Center.

Perez, W., Espinoza, R., Ramos, K., Coronado, H., & Cortes, R. (2009). Academic resilience among undocumented Latino students. *Hispanic Journal of Behavioral Sciences*, 31, 149–181.

Perez Huber, L., Benavides, C., Malagon, M., Velez, V., & Solorzano, D. (2008). Getting beyond the 'symptom,' acknowledging the 'disease': Theorizing racist nativism. *Contemporary Justice Review*, 11, 39–51.

Perez Huber, L., & Malagon, M. (2007). Silenced struggles: The experiences of Latina and Latino undocumented college students in California. *Nevada Law Journal*, 7, 841–861.

Perez Huber, L., Malagon, M., & Solorzano, D. (May 2009). *Struggling for opportunity: Undocumented AB 540 students in the Latina/o Education pipeline*. Research Report No. 13. UCLA Chicano Studies Research Center.

Perez Huber, L., Huidor, O., Malagon, M., & Solorzano, D. (March 2006). *Falling through the cracks: Critical transitions in the Latina/o Educational pipeline*, Research Report No. 7. UCLA Chicano Studies Research Center.

Rangel, Y. (2001). *College immigrant students: How undocumented female Mexican immigrant students transition into higher education*. Unpublished doctoral dissertation, University of California, Los Angeles.

UCLA Center for Labor Research and Education. (2008). *Underground undergrads: UCLA undocumented immigrant students speak out*. Los Angeles: UCLA Center for Labor Research and Education.

U.S. Bureau of the Census. (2004). United States selected population profile, total population, 2004 American Community Survey. Retrieved March 18, 2009, from www.factfinder.census.gov.

Velez, V., Perez Huber, L., Benavides, C., de la Luz, A., & Solorzano, D. (2008). Battling for human rights and social justice: A Latina/o critical race analysis of Latina/o student youth activism in the wake of 2006 anti-immigrant sentiment. *Social Justice, 35*, 7–27.

Yosso, T. (2005). Whose culture has capital? A critical race theory discussion of community cultural wealth. *Race Ethnicity and Education, 8*, 69–91.

Yosso, T. (2006). *Critical race counterstories along the Chicana/Chicano educational pipeline.* New York: Routledge.

Yosso, T., & Solorzano, D. (March 2006). *Leaks in the Chicana and Chicano educational pipeline.* Latino Policy & Issues Brief No. 13, UCLA Chicano Studies Research Center.

INTRODUCTION

"I see my illegal status as a wall . . . if I were to get deported I would be an alien in my own country . . . we are humans and we have families and we have feelings . . . they should see the good stuff in us."

—Jairo, Community College Student

"Even though I worked extremely hard I have to work twice as hard to go beyond high school . . . I have a drive to do better, to work hard, and to contribute but I just don't have the means to do it. . . . This is our home and we're ready to contribute."

—Sasha, University Student

W HEN I began interviewing undocumented students in the spring of 2006, I wanted to better understand their educational experiences. My goal was to learn about their experiences growing up "American." Although I was expecting the usual list of school activities, I did not expect the high levels of community service and volunteering that they reported. This trend was particularly remarkable because these youth are so marginalized in our society. They have almost no legal rights, they can be deported at any time, they are not eligible for most government services, they cannot legally work, and, most frustrating of all, they are not eligible for financial aid to attend college. So I started to wonder: What motivates these marginalized young adults to be so civically involved? Why are they devoted to a society that shuns them socially and politically?

This book is a compilation of the inspiring and untold stories of 16 students who are currently undocumented and of 4 others who lived a significant proportion of their lives undocumented, but who now have legalized their status. In their own words, undocumented students reflect on their hardships, accomplishments, dreams, ambitions, and desire to be accepted as regular Americans. Their parents brought them to this country when they were infants in most cases, and for many of them, this country is the only home they know. They have grown up "American" in every way possible; their dominant language is English, they proclaim an American identity, and they live an American lifestyle. In various ways, their community service participation and activities reinforce their affinity toward American society.

Judged by their appearance, undocumented high school seniors are indistinguishable from their U.S.-born classmates. They wear the same jeans and T-shirts and mingle in the hallways between classes gossiping and joking with their friends. These students enjoy the right to a public education in the United States that provides them—just like citizen and legal resident students—with a social center, a place to learn, an affordable lunch, and the chance to join a club or a sports team, or to play in the band. The similarities begin to dissolve, however, if you ask any of them to talk candidly about their outlook on the future and their possibilities after high school. After graduation day, the harsh reality sets in, that even though they worked hard to excel in school, their options to pursue higher education are limited because of their undocumented status.

The students I had the privilege of interviewing exhibit the same type of optimism that fueled their parents' desire to pursue a better future in the United States. Despite the numerous social, political, economic, and educational challenges they face, undocumented youth demonstrate tenacious optimism, drive, and perseverance in the face of societal marginalization. The United States has provided them with educational access first guaranteed by the 1982 landmark Supreme Court case of *Plyer v. Doe*, in which the court ruled that all children, regardless of their immigration status, have a right to a basic education. Since the *Plyer* decision, hundreds of thousands of undocumented students have come of age and graduated from American high schools, looking toward the next level of educational opportunity. Upon graduating however, these "college-eligible" students are unable to pursue higher education due to their lack of legal status, current federal law, and limited financial resources.

Since 2000, increasing numbers of newspaper stories all over the country have chronicled the struggles of undocumented students who believed in and aspired to achieve the American dream, only to learn upon their high school graduation that the American dream precludes them. One of these students was Jesus Apodaca, an 18-year-old undocumented student who on August 11, 2002, was featured in a *Denver Post* story about how federal law prevents schools from offering financial aid or in-state tuition to undocumented students. After reading the story, then U.S. representative for the state of Colorado, Tom Tancredo, contacted the U.S. Immigration and Naturalization Service in Denver and asked that Apodaca and any of his undocumented relatives be deported. In another example, in May 2005, the *Chicago Reporter* ran a similar story about a talented undocumented student named Sarahy. Five years earlier, her parents had brought her to the United States from Mexico. In high school, she maintained a 3.8 grade point average, was extensively involved in the dance program, and volunteered at a local community organization. Her accomplishments led to admission at her dream school, Loyola University Chicago. Because of her undocumented status, however, she was not eligible for any form of financial aid or on-campus job. With no other way to offset the cost—Loyola's tuition was beyond her family's economic means—she could not attend, shattering her dream.

These and dozens of other newspaper stories highlight that although undocumented youths have grown up as Americans, they have lived as outsiders with restricted access to the basic resources and institutions most Americans would deem essential for survival and success. These include driver's licenses, the opportunity for legal employment, and financial aid for college. Many undocumented immigrants have no choice but to work in the cash-based economy, and the only option they have to fund their college pursuits is a limited number of private scholarships. Consequently, most undocumented youths live in hiding as they and their families are in constant fear of being discovered and deported back to their countries of origin—countries that many have not seen for more than a decade and with which they now have little or no familiarity.

The U.S. Supreme Court mandates that undocumented children be accepted as students, but because of current immigration laws, they are not accepted as citizens. This puts these students in an ambiguous situation that raises some very important questions: How are they responding? Do they sink to the bottom, resent the culture, and consider going back to their country of birth? Or do they take courage somehow, find hope, and rise to the very top? The amazing and inspiring stories in this book suggest that undocumented immigrant students' lack of access to citizenship and higher education represents a civil rights and social justice travesty as well as an ongoing loss of intellectual and civic talent to American society. Their stories document many of the deep flaws of failed immigration and education policies in the United States and the subsequent impact on undocumented students and their families. We ARE Americans links the experiences of undocumented students to larger social and policy issues of immigration reform, social and political marginalization, and access to higher education.

Changing Demographics

Failed immigration policies, as well as economic push-and-pull factors have played a central role in increasing the undocumented population in the United States to approximately 12 million as of 2006.[1] California is home to the highest number of undocumented residents, with an estimated 2.8 million; followed by Texas, with nearly 1.4 million; and Florida, with 850,000.[2] As their numbers have increased over the years, hostile media images of undocumented immigrants, scapegoating of immigrants by politicians, and anti-immigrant rhetoric by nativist groups have led to persistent negative public opinion about undocumented immigrants.

In 2002, the National Survey of Latinos[3] indicated that 71% of Latinos felt that undocumented immigrants help the economy, compared to 26% of Whites and 26% of Blacks. In addition, whereas 90% of Latinos favor legalizing undocumented immigrants, only 66% of Whites and 67% of Blacks also favored legalization, while only 8% of Latinos oppose it, compared to 30% of Whites and 33% of Blacks. Despite persistent negative public opinion and negative media images, the research suggests that immigrants: (1) contribute to the economy, (2) do not strain social services, (3) and are not prone to criminal activity.

Economic Contributions of Undocumented Immigrants

A perception that drives hostile public opinion about undocumented immigrants is that they are exploiting the U.S. economy. The widespread belief is that the undocumented cost more in government services than they contribute to the economy. This belief is demonstrably false as noted by almost every empirical study on the economic impact of undocumented immigrants. The research documents the exact opposite, that the undocumented actually contribute more to public coffers in taxes than they cost in social services.[4] Their labor brings down the costs of goods and services for all and makes firms and sometimes entire industries more competitive.

The benefits to the overall economy are several. Restaurant prices are pushed down by undocumented labor in the kitchen, low fruit and vegetable prices by undocumented field hands, and new-home prices by undocumented construction workers. The tens of thousands of undocumented nannies in the Los Angeles area lower the cost of child care, freeing many mothers to return to work. This in turn increases families' incomes, which encourages spending and fuels the economy.[5] Many immigrants send a portion of their earnings home to their families, but their influence here remains potent. The Economic Roundtable, a Los Angeles think tank, estimates that the 400,000 undocumented workers in Los Angeles County spend $5.7 billion annually on food, rent, transportation, and other necessities. The sales tax immigrants pay on all consumer purchases boosts the state treasury. There are also many undocumented workers with payroll jobs who contribute to Social Security without the right to receive payments from the fund. The U.S. Social Security Trust Fund reported a surplus of more than $49 billion in 2000 from payroll collections from persons with invalid Social Security identification numbers.[6]

A 2006 study by the Texas State comptroller found that the estimated 1.4 million undocumented immigrants in Texas in fiscal year 2005 added

$17.7 billion to the gross state product. Undocumented immigrants produced $1.58 billion in state revenues for Texas, which *exceeded* the $1.16 billion in state services they received.[7] Similarly, a 2007 Oregon Center for Public Policy study estimated that undocumented immigrants in Oregon pay state income, excise, and property taxes as well as federal Social Security and Medicare taxes, which total between $134 million and $187 million annually, with an additional $97 million to $136 million paid in taxes annually by Oregon employers on behalf of undocumented workers. Undocumented workers are not able to draw on those contributions since they are ineligible for the Oregon Health Plan, food stamps, and temporary cash assistance.[8] In Iowa, a 2007 report by the Iowa Policy Project concluded that undocumented immigrants pay an estimated $40 million to $62 million in state taxes each year, with an additional estimated $50 million to $77.8 million in federal Social Security and Medicare taxes paid by undocumented immigrants and their employers.[9] Due to their status, these Iowa workers will never benefit from those contributions. Thus, rather than draining state resources, undocumented immigrants are in some cases *subsidizing* services that only documented residents can access.

In addition to their tax contributions, the consumer purchasing power of undocumented immigrants—what they spend on goods, services, and housing—not only creates new jobs, but also provides federal, state, and local governments with additional revenue through sales, income, business, and property taxes. In other words, spending by undocumented immigrants has an economic "multiplier effect." For instance, a 2002 study by the Center for Urban Economic Development at the University of Chicago found that undocumented immigrants in the Chicago metropolitan area alone spent $2.89 billion in 2001. These expenditures stimulated an additional $2.56 billion in local spending, for a total of $5.45 billion in additional spending, or 1.5% of the gross regional product. This spending, in turn, sustained 31,908 jobs in the local economy.[10]

Use of Public Services

Another widespread misconception about undocumented immigrants is that they burden public service agencies. Again, the research refutes this.

In California, the state with the largest undocumented population, the research indicates that undocumented residents not only use fewer health services than do citizens and documented residents, they also tend to be younger and healthier than the average Californian. When they do use health services, undocumented immigrants are less reliant on public funds (such as Medicare and Medicaid) to pay for their care[11] and instead primarily pay out-of-pocket costs for health care. For example, of the $430 billion in national medical spending in 2000, native-born residents accounted for 87% of the population, but for 91.5% of the spending. Undocumented immigrants—3.2% of the population—accounted for only about 1.5% of medical costs.[12]

Crime

Undocumented immigrants are also falsely presumed to be prone to criminal activity, a perception that is not consistent with actual crime statistics. For instance, a 2008 report by the Immigration Policy Center (IPC)[13] documents numerous studies that indicate immigrants are *less* likely to commit crimes or be behind bars than are the native-born, and high rates of immigration are *not* associated with higher rates of crime. Although the undocumented immigrant population *doubled* to about 12 million between 1994 and 2004, IPC cites data from the Bureau of Justice Statistics that indicate that the violent crime rate in the United States *declined* by 35.1% during this time, and the property crime rate fell by 25%. The decline in crime rates was not just national, but also occurred in border cities and in other cities with large immigrant populations such as San Diego, El Paso, Los Angeles, New York, Chicago, and Miami. According to a 2008 report from the conservative Americas Majority Foundation, crime rates are *lowest* in states with the *highest* immigration growth rates. The study found that from 1999 to 2006, the total crime rate declined 13.6% in the 19 highest-immigration states, compared to a 7.1% decline in the other 32 states, including Washington, DC. Also, in 2006, the 10 "high influx" states—those with the most dramatic, recent increases in immigration—had the lowest rates of violent crime and total crime.[14]

An analysis of data from the New Jersey Department of Corrections and U.S. Census Bureau by New Jersey's *Star-Ledger* found that while non-U.S. citizens comprise 10% of the state's overall population, they account for 5% of the 22,623 inmates in prison in 2007. Finally, a 2008 report from the Public Policy Institute of California found that the incarceration rate for foreign-born adults is 297 per 100,000 in the population, compared to 813 per 100,000 for U.S.-born adults. The foreign-born, who make up roughly 35% of California's adult population, constitute 17% of the state prison population, a proportion that has remained fairly constant since 1990.[15]

Whereas some have noted the number of undocumented immigrants in federal detention centers, reporting of these figures often fails to mention that violations of U.S. immigration law are civil infractions, not criminal acts, and most violators are guilty only of seeking to improve their welfare, and that of their families, by taking jobs that few Americans want. Upon arriving in the United States, they begin to set roots in their communities and enroll their children in school, thus exercising their children's right to a public education, as declared by the 1982 landmark Supreme Court case of *Plyer v. Doe*.

Plyer v. Doe

The constitutional right to a public education for undocumented students emerged from one of the first well-known attempts to limit undocumented students' access to public education. In 1975, the Texas Legislature passed a law (Texas Education Code, Section 21.031) that denied undocumented immigrants access to public schools by withholding funds from school districts that enrolled undocumented children. This law also allowed public schools to demand proof of citizenship and to deny admission to those who could not verify their legal status in this country. A series of local lawsuits successfully challenged the constitutionality of that law, and in 1982 the U.S. Supreme Court established the right of undocumented children to a public education. The *Plyer v. Doe* decision noted that the Equal Protection Clause of the Fourteenth

Amendment also protected undocumented immigrants. The use of constitutional guarantees to reaffirm students' rights makes *Plyer v. Doe* a key decision on behalf of immigrants' rights in the United States.[16]

Undocumented Students Today

Currently, the *Plyer* decision protects the educational rights of approximately 1.8 million children under 18 years of age, about one-sixth of the total undocumented population.[17] Their educational rights expire once they're beyond compulsory schooling age, as is the case for the estimated 3.4 million undocumented young adults between the ages of 18 and 29. Higher education is an elusive dream for these young adults, with only 10% of undocumented males and 16% of undocumented females ages 18 to 24 enrolled in college.[18]

An estimated 65,000 undocumented students graduate from the nation's high schools each year.[19] About two-thirds are of Latino descent, and 40% live in California. Tragically, only about 10% to 20% of undocumented youth who graduate from high school go on to college, with estimates ranging between 7,000 and 13,000.[20] In California, approximately 25,000 undocumented students graduate from high school each year, yet fewer than 7,000 enroll in community colleges, with much lower enrollment figures for the University of California and the California State University systems.[21]

Higher Education Access and In-State Tuition Legislation

Increased media attention regarding the plight of undocumented high school graduates unable to pursue higher education, and the brave efforts of advocates in collaboration with state legislators, led to the nation's first state law in support of college-going undocumented students. In 2001, Texas governor Rick Perry signed into law state HB 1403, a bill spearheaded by State Representative Rick Noriega that allowed undocumented Texas high school graduates to pay in-state tuition at public colleges and universities. To gain broad support for the bill, advocates relied primarily on an economic rationale: the bill would increase enrollment of, and fees from, students who otherwise would not enroll or would drop out. In addition, The Texas State comptroller conducted an economic impact study that concluded that every dollar the state invested in higher education for undocumented students would yield more than five dollars for the Texas economy in the long run.[22] Following the Texas example, and relying on a similar economic rationale, California passed its own in-state tuition bill for undocumented California high school graduates, AB540, in 2001. Similar to the Texas legislation, the California bill permits students who complete three years or more of high school in California to qualify for in-state tuition. As of 2009, eight other states have passed in-state tuition legislation for undocumented students, with Texas, Oklahoma, and New Mexico also providing access to state grants to pay for tuition costs.

In-state legislation has increased the number of undocumented students pursuing a college degree, but enrollment figures are modest at best. In California, estimates suggest that in 2005 about 1,620 undocumented students were enrolled in the University of California and California State University systems under AB540. While this number does not include community colleges, where the majority of undocumented students matriculate, it is only a fraction of the 2.5 million students enrolled in California higher education institutions—208,000 in the University of California system alone.[23]

Similarly, an increasing number of undocumented Texas students have taken advantage of the in-state tuition program, although they account for only a small portion of the state's 1 million-plus enrolled in higher education. In the fall of 2005, nearly 5,100 undocumented students enrolled under Texas's in-state tuition law, up from 400 students during the first year of the program. Nearly 80% of all undocumented students who were enrolled in 2005 attended community colleges.[24]

In other states, the number of undocumented students enrolled in college under in-state tuition legislation is significantly lower. In 2005, Kansas saw 221 undocumented students enroll in Kansas public colleges, while the University of New Mexico system saw 41 undocumented students enroll that semester. Twenty-seven were admitted to the University of Washington system, while at the University of Utah, 22 were enrolled. In 2006, an estimated 100 undocumented students enrolled in public Massachusetts colleges.[25] Numbers are not available for Illinois, New York, or Oklahoma, but comparable enrollments are suspected. Despite the modest but increasing numbers of undocumented students enrolling in college and completing their degrees, a major hurdle remains; they are not legally able to put their college degree to work. Without federal legislation legalizing their status, their future remains uncertain. Since 2001, Congress has tried to address their legal limbo with the introduction of the DREAM Act.

The DREAM Act

On May 21, 2001, Reps. Lucille Roybal-Allard (D-CA), Christopher Cannon (R-UT), and Howard Berman (D-CA) introduced in the U.S. House of Representatives the Student Adjustment Act of 2001 (H.R. 1918), while the Senate version, the Development, Relief and Education for Alien Minors (DREAM) Act (S. 1291), was introduced on August 1, 2001, by Sen. Orrin Hatch (R-UT). The bill was placed on the Senate legislative calendar but never received a floor vote. The DREAM Act (S. 2075) was introduced again in the U.S. Senate in November 2005, followed by the 2006 New American Dream Act (H.R. 5131) introduced in the U.S. House of Representatives. On May 25, 2006, the U.S. Senate reached a bipartisan compromise on comprehensive immigration reform and passed a landmark immigration bill (S. 2611) that incorporated the DREAM Act. The bill did not receive the necessary votes to be sent to President George W. Bush. The bill was reintroduced on March 26, 2009, as the DREAM Act (S.720) in the Senate by Dick Durbin (D-IL) and Richard Lugar (R-IN), and it was introduced that same day in the House of Representatives as the American Dream Act by Howard Berman (D-CA), Lincoln Diaz-Balart (R-FL), and Lucille Roybal-Allard (D-CA).

Although there have been some modifications from initial introduction of the bill, the DREAM Act would extend a six-year conditional legal status to undocumented youth who meet several criteria, including:

♦ entry into the United States before age 16;

♦ continuous presence in the United States for five years prior to the bill's enactment;

♦ receipt of a high school diploma or its equivalent (i.e., a GED); and

♦ demonstrated good moral character.

Qualifying youth would be authorized to work in the United States, go to school, or join the military. If during the six-year period they graduate from a two-year college, complete at least two years of a four-year degree, or serve at least two years in the U.S. military, the beneficiary would be able to adjust from conditional to permanent legal resident status. Otherwise, after six years, their conditional status would lapse. Making legal status conditional on young adults' educational and military choices has no precedent in U.S. immigration policy.

Without federal legislation, state efforts to support undocumented students can provide only temporary relief. Congress must provide a path to legalization for undocumented students. It does not make sense for states to pay for postsecondary education only to have those students forbidden to work legally in the United States upon graduation. Even though the states are taking steps in the right direction, their hands are tied until Congress allows undocumented students to legalize their status.[26]

From an economic perspective, legalizing undocumented students could be a significant incentive for them to work harder to graduate from high school, thus improving their odds of getting a higher education, which ultimately would increase tax revenues from the higher salaries of increasing numbers of college graduates. The increased fiscal contribution would easily repay the required educational investment within a few years and, thereafter, would provide a profit to taxpayers for several decades. The impact of legalization would not be limited to increased earnings, tax revenues, and social services savings. In a stable economy, such legalization would enable thousands of young immigrants to join the legal workforce, helping businesses and the economy fill crucial needs. Under current law, they are forced to work illegally in the cash economy as domestic workers, day laborers, ambulatory sellers, and sweatshop factory workers. In difficult economic times, they can make a much needed contribution, as attested by Alba (chapter 16), who is ready to fill the urgent need for math teachers in our school systems, and by Julia (chapter 18), who intends to use her doctorate in engineering to teach and foster new talent. By encouraging more of these students to study the sciences and engineering, they can contribute to our future competitiveness as a nation.

One particular concern about legalizing undocumented students is that it could take away seats in colleges and universities, as well as financial aid, from native-born students who want to pursue postsecondary education. However, this fear is not substantiated by the experiences of the 10 states that have passed laws allowing undocumented students who are in-state high school graduates to qualify for in-state college tuition. As already noted, these states (California, Illinois, Kansas, Nebraska, New Mexico, New York, Oklahoma, Texas, Utah, and Washington), which are home to about half of the nation's undocumented immigrants, have not experienced a large influx of undocumented student enrollment in higher education, have not had to displace any native-born students, or had undocumented students be a financial drain on their educational systems.[27] Even if their numbers were to rise, on the basis of the statistical evidence already demonstrated about the net contribution of the undocumented population, and on the anecdotal evidence of the stories in this book, they are likely to make a very positive contribution to the overall economy.

National Self-Interest of Integrating Students into Society

The Acculturation Rationale

The American economy asked for workers, and with them came families and children who now call cities across the country home. The debate so far has relied mostly on stereotypes and misconceptions about unauthorized immigrants—as workers and taxpayers on the positive side, or as lawbreakers and service abusers on the negative side—but the debate has not been well informed by research on the characteristics of the unauthorized population.[28]

The overwhelming majority of undocumented children and young adults have grown up in the United States, attended U.S. schools, and lived in the country for virtually all of their lives. Since they were raised in the United States during their formative years, they consider themselves Americans. In fact, most know no culture other than that of the United States, as their ties with their native countries were severed years ago when they left with their parents. Socially, they are indisputably full-fledged members of U.S. society, even if they are only on the lower rungs of the socioeconomic ladder. After having been educated in our schools, they speak English (often with more ease than they do Spanish), envision their futures here, and have internalized U.S. values and expectations of merit; yet they have no available paths for formal legal integration. Paradoxically, their efforts to adapt and contribute economically are met with legal obstacles. Rather than valuing these youth as important societal resources, current policies restrict their options and curb the transformative potential undocumented youth have in their communities. Without full legal rights, undocumented youth will be barred from the traditional paths of upward mobility available to other immigrants throughout U.S. history. These young adults deserve immediate legalization so they can pursue their lives in the United States as full-fledged Americans.

If the United States does not enforce immigration laws with employers, then it must deal with the consequences of immigrants' acculturation in society. The government cannot allow the business sector to entice workers to the country, benefit from their labor, ignore employment and immigration laws, and then deny these workers the rights, social services, benefits, and protections available to all other workers and their families. Undocumented workers bring their families, join relatives, and enroll their children in schools where they live as they take available jobs in the market. They lay down roots, become invested, and contribute socially and civically in their communities. Thus, enforcement of immigration policies must take into account these forms of social and civic investment on the part of the millions of long-term undocumented immigrants. By denying benefits to long-term undocumented workers we violate our normative principles of unity, community, and equality and discriminate against noncitizens who contribute to the overall well-being of society just as much as citizens.

The Economic Rationale

The United States of America was founded upon the notion that achievement should trump social status. Many undocumented students have worked hard to overcome poverty to become valedictorians, athletes, artists, and academic champions. They attend schools that lack books and other educational supplies, advanced placement classes, and functional bathrooms, yet they manage to earn stellar grades and gain acceptance to top universities. The better policy is to view them as valuable resources for our nation's future instead of depriving them of the means by which they can improve their lives and, thereby, improve society. The progressive approach is one that accepts the reality of the undocumented population and demands that the federal government afford them the ability to become productive members of society. Otherwise, the inescapable reality for undocumented students is that without the prospect of normalizing their immigration status, the education they receive is useful for personal growth, but is of little consequence because they remain unable to participate in our democratic society. From an economic standpoint, denying legal status to undocumented students creates a subclass of citizens who otherwise are fully capable of becoming successful individuals (i.e., skilled professionals) and, thus, significant taxpayers. Without legalization, undocumented students are permanently locked into the lowest socioeconomic class, perpetuating poverty among immigrant communities.

Two-thirds of all immigrants live in six states: California, Florida, Illinois, New Jersey, New York, and Texas. These states in particular have much to gain economically from their population of undocumented students. They have invested state resources in educating them up to the high school level and have nurtured them into becoming self-sustaining individuals. Without legalizing undocumented students, these states cannot get the return on their educational investment.

At a bare minimum, the economic and social realities of the 21st century demand college completion. A high school diploma simply does not grant access to jobs that generate the type of income correlated with individual achievement and success. There is a growing gap between the annual earnings of those with just a high school diploma and those with a postsecondary education. In 1975, full-time, year-round workers with a bachelor's degree had 1.5 times the annual earnings of workers with only a high school diploma. That ratio rose to 1.8 by 1999. Furthermore, in 2002 the average earnings ranged from $18,900 for high school dropouts to $25,900 for high school graduates, $45,000 for college graduates, and $99,300 for workers with professional degrees.[29] Finally, according to the Bureau of Labor Statistics (BLS),[30] workers who lacked a high school diploma in 2006 earned an average of only $419 per week and had an unemployment rate of 6.8%. In contrast, workers with a bachelor's degree earned $962 per week and had an unemployment rate of 2.3%, while those with a doctorate earned $1,441 and had an unemployment rate of only 1.4%. These data suggest that the skills associated with postsecondary education as well as credentials provide access to individual economic freedom. Moreover, postsecondary schooling equips people with higher-order skills, which increase their chances of getting a higher-paying job. Denying legalization to long-term undocumented residents of our states will economically disadvantage those individuals and the communities in which they live. All of this accentuates the importance of access to postsecondary education for all substantive members, including undocumented students.

Would legalizing undocumented youth create a system too open for us to control, administer, or pay for? Most people recognize that any type of mass exodus of undocumented immigrants would wreak economic havoc on major industries.[31] Furthermore, most of the limited-resource arguments against undocumented immigrant access to various social goods understate tax collections from immigrants; overstate service costs for immigrants; do not consider the range of economic benefits of undocumented labor, spending, and business; exaggerate job displacement of native workers; neglect to show that native-born workers often consume more services than they pay in taxes; and overestimate the size of the immigrant population.[32]

Regularization Efforts

Many elected officials, as well as public opinion, do not support legislation that would legalize undocumented immigrants. Many point to the inability of the 1986 Immigration Reform and Control Act (IRCA) to stem the flow of undocumented immigrants. What critics often fail to mention, however, is that IRCA greatly facilitated the economic integration of undocumented workers. Most of the unauthorized immigrants who obtained legal status in 1986 under IRCA had found better jobs by 1992 than the ones they secured when they arrived. As a group, most but not all of the unauthorized immigrants who were legalized through IRCA arrived with relatively low skill levels and found low-skill, low-wage jobs. Yet, by 1992, five years after legalization, most had jobs that were better than the first jobs they reported and, for many, much better than the jobs they had in their homeland. In short, they had improved their status as a result of unauthorized immigration and legalization.[33] Given the opportunity to receive additional education and training and move into better-paying jobs, legalized immigrants pay more in taxes and have more money to spend and invest.

Lessons learned from IRCA suggest that instead of seeking perfect legislation, with its predictable disappointments, controlling unauthorized immigration might proceed from the twin premises that uncertainty and imperfection will be a way of life, and policies will always be partly an exercise in the inexact. To deal with this reality, channeling unauthorized immigration into regulated pathways might be a more realistic course than current policy goals, which seek total control or exclusion—goals that tend to create unrealistic public expectations and fuel further intolerance.[34] Extraordinary regularization programs granting legal status to unauthorized immigrants, such as IRCA, are not a new phenomenon, nor are they limited to the United States. Countries that have instituted such programs in the last quarter-century include Canada, Belgium, France, Italy, Spain, Greece, Portugal, Argentina, Venezuela, and the United Kingdom.[35] In southern Europe specifically, Italy, Spain, Greece, and Portugal have repeatedly conducted regularizations of their unauthorized populations—completing a total of 14 programs in the past two decades.

The regularization of unauthorized immigrants, while controversial and politically complicated, is a public policy challenge that we cannot ignore or ever perfect. Still, there remains a host of ways regularization can be made into a more effective migration management policy tool. Regularization not only prevents the population of unauthorized resident immigrants from building to high levels, it can also make management of migration more effective when used in concert with other migration management strategies, such as greater openings to legal migration, and more honest cooperation with sending and transit countries; earned regularization that uses tough but fair and transparent criteria can set the stage for better policy development and smarter use of enforcement resources.[36] Properly conceived and carefully executed regularization programs have the potential to become an investment in more orderly labor markets, in the rule of law, and in social stability through inclusion while meeting important security, labor market, and social policy goals.

Constitutional and Moral Rationale

Opposition to immigration is not new. Throughout U.S. history, some people have opposed the influx of immigrants from around the world who came here to find a better life. They protested against the Italians, Germans, Greeks, and Irish. They were so concerned about the number of Chinese "coolies" that they forced legislation to keep them out. Opponents were up in arms over Scandinavians, Japanese, Koreans, and Vietnamese. They worried about the number of "foreigners" coming from Central and South America. Yet the United States ultimately made a place for these immigrants and was enriched by their cultural contributions, talents, and hard work.

Despite widespread misconceptions, there are not more immigrants now than during any previous period of American history. The foreign-born population in the country, estimated at about 37.5 million in 2006, is only about 12.5% of the national population.[37] This figure is lower than the percentage of U.S. population that was foreign-born between 1860 and 1920, which ranged between 13.2% and 14.8%.[38] Whether motivated by fear, prejudice, or honest concerns, the debate over whether undocumented residents should be allowed in this country is a moot point. Rounding up and deporting 12 million undocumented immigrants who own property in this country, and whose children are U.S. citizens, would violate all of the fundamental values and ideals on which our country was built. We must not forget the ideals and values that gave birth to this country: *freedom, equality, independence*. As we begin our immigration reform efforts, we must remain committed to our time-honored values. We must not lash out irrationally against hard-working and decent human beings, but, instead, we must remain faithful to those ideals.

I am not suggesting that we subvert the immigration admissions process. The establishment of procedures for the entry and removal of migration flows are necessary and legitimate. Instead, I argue that laws regarding admission cannot be enforced or implemented in ways that transform immigrants into pariahs. In the process of developing appropriate enforcement of immigration flows at all ports of entry, we must adhere to equity in our treatment of undocumented immigrants who already live in the United States. Subjugating undocumented immigrants who are long-term residents undermines the preservation of our society as a community of equals. Immigration laws can be enforced by better regulation at points of entry and well-developed sanctions, not by imposing social disabilities. Denying established immigrant residents the rights and recognition of membership misrepresents the American constitutional tradition, which is concerned with protecting "persons," a category that includes aliens and citizens. We must stop the continued subordination of undocumented persons.

Millions of people are disenfranchised because they cannot become citizens in their countries of residence. If democracy is to be maintained and enhanced, all members of society must have a political voice as citizens. Citizenship must take into account not only residence within a state's territory, but also other significant links such as family bonds, economic involvement, or cultural participation. Citizenship rules must recognize that individuality is always formed in social and cultural contexts, and in the case of long-term undocumented residents, they have been shaped by the American social and cultural context and, thus, they have become members of our social and cultural groups.

Undocumented youths and their families live among us and often have formed family and community connections. Formal exclusion of undocumented youth from our rich traditions of constitutional discourse also risks the creation of a subcaste group. It also facilitates irrational discrimination against the undocumented who live, work, pay taxes, raise children, and participate in communities alongside citizens every day. The stories in this book strongly suggest that the rights of the undocumented should be clearer and grounded more in mainstream constitutional norms, more in their humanity than in their immigration status. Lack of legal status renders immigrants not simply foreigners, it brands them as criminals, subject to expulsion—as no less than complete outcasts. Under the current system, length of residence is irrelevant, family ties here are meaningless, and hardship is immaterial. In an increasingly global world, the current basis of citizenship rights seems a rigid, vestigial relic.

To what extent should the constitution protect undocumented young adults in the United States? I argue that the best reading of the constitution is one that provides as much parity as possible between citizen and noncitizen, regardless of formal immigration status. We should welcome undocumented persons. We have recruited and relied on them for generations; they have contributed to the economic greatness of our country; and their children have become part of the social fabric of our nation. Like newcomers of the past, they are here to seek a better life through hard work and dedication to their families. Welcoming them is the right thing to do.

Showing compassion and fairness in our immigration policies is not a sign of weakness or a lack of reason. Rather, those traits demonstrate confidence in a rule of law and a system of government that metes out punishment when necessary but understands that regulating the lives of those who seek to live within our borders must be done with the upmost compassion, dignity, and understanding. As in previous generations, there is much to admire about individuals who come to America seeking freedom and a better life. Let us welcome undocumented youths and their families into our society so they can contribute more fully to their communities. This is how we continue to build our nation of immigrants in a just, humane, intelligent, and moral manner. This is how we fulfill our commitment to a policy of humanity.

In this introduction, I have summarized much of the compelling evidence that suggests that Congress needs to address the tentative situation of millions of young people who are hostages of a confusing and contradictory immigration system. In school we encourage students to aspire to greatness, yet we deny undocumented students the opportunity to share in the so-called American dream. Can we really afford to waste such a valuable national resource?

Organization of the Book

The collection of personal narratives in this book was drawn from in-depth interviews with undocumented students from diverse educational settings that included public high schools, community colleges, state universities, private universities, and highly selective four-year institutions in Arizona, California, Colorado, the District of Columbia, Georgia, Illinois, Missouri, New Mexico, New York, Texas, Virginia, and Washington. In the course of the interviews, I conducted additional field observations and informal interviews with teachers and members of grassroots and student organizations that advocate on behalf of undocumented students. These various sources of information provided me with multiple perspectives and a deeper understanding of the social and educational experiences of undocumented students.

Each of the first four chapters provides a biographical sketch and educational history of four undocumented high school students. These students are on the cusp of graduating and are dealing with the pending disappointment and uncertainty regarding their future college plans. The next four chapters, in part two, focus on undocumented students who have embarked on an uncertain voyage in their quest for a college education. These students have begun their journey at community colleges due to their affordable tuition rates. Some of the students in these stories were accepted to a four-year university, but the high cost of tuition placed their dream out of reach, leaving them with no choice but to take the long route while confronting ongoing social, legal, economic, and educational challenges. The chapters in part three tell the stories of four undocumented university students who face increasing economic challenges and experience growing despair as they approach their highly coveted goal of a college degree with the bittersweet feeling that such an attainment will do little to alleviate their ongoing marginality. Part four highlights the resilience and resourcefulness of undocumented college graduates who refuse to give up and continue to remain optimistic about the possibility of becoming full-fledged legal citizens. They hope and are actively involved in political activism that advocates for the rights of undocumented immigrants, while at the same time they are continuing their education by enrolling part time in graduate degree programs. Finally, part five provides insight into how markedly different the lives of undocumented students would be if they were to become legalized. These four chapters focus on four individuals who lived most of their lives being undocumented, but whose lives changed overnight when they legalized their status. These individuals were able to realize their dreams and became civically engaged doctors, lawyers, and educators. Finally, the conclusion revisits the overall rationale for immediate federal legislation to legalize undocumented students and provides several resources and suggestions for individuals who wish to advocate for more equitable immigration and education laws.

Notes

1. Passel, J. S. (2006). *The size and characteristics of the unauthorized migration population in the U.S.: Estimates based on the March 2005 Current Population Survey*. Washington, DC: Pew Hispanic Center.

2. Hoefer, M., Rytina, N., & Campbell, C. (2006). *Estimates of the unauthorized immigrant population residing in the United States: January 2005*. Washington, DC: Department of Homeland Security, Office of Immigration Statistics.

3. Pew Hispanic Center. (2004). *The 2002 National Survey of Latinos*. Washington, DC: Author.

4. Lipman, F. J. (2006). Taxing undocumented immigrants: Separate, inequal and without representation. *Harvard Latino Law Review, 9*, 1–58.

5. Orrenius, P. M., & Zavodny, M. (2004). What are the consequences of an amnesty for undocumented immigrants? *Federal Reserve Bank of Atlanta Working Paper Series, 2004–10*.

6. Social Security Administration. (2002). *Congressional response report: Status of the Social Security Administration's Earnings Suspense File*. Washington, DC: Author.

7. Strayhorn, C. K. (2006). *Special report: Undocumented immigrants in Texas: A financial analysis of the impact to the state budget and economy*. Austin, TX: Office of the Texas State Comptroller.

8. Oregon Center for Public Policy. (2007). *Undocumented workers are taxpayers, too*. Silverton, OR: Author.

9. Pearson, B., & Sheehan, M. F. (2007). *Undocumented Immigrants in Iowa: Estimated tax contributions and fiscal impact.* Mt. Vernon, IA: The Iowa Policy Project.

10. Mehta, C., Theodore, N., Mora, I., & Wade, J. (2002). *Chicago's undocumented immigrants: An analysis of wages, working conditions, and economic contributions.* Chicago: Center for Urban Economic Development.

11. California Health Care Foundation. (2007). *Are undocumented residents a major drain on public and private health care resources?* Oakland, CA: Author.

12. Goldman, D., Smith, J. P., & Sood, N. (2006). *The public spends little to provide health care for undocumented immigrants.* Santa Monica, CA: RAND.

13. Immigration Policy Center. (2008). *From anecdotes to evidence: Setting the record straight on immigrants and crime.* Washington, DC: Author.

14. Nadler, R. (2008). *Immigration and the wealth of states.* Overland Park, KS: Americas Majority Foundation.

15. Butcher, K., & Piehl, A. M. (2008). *Crime, corrections, and California: What does immigration have to do with it?* San Francisco: Public Policy Institute of California.

16. Olivas, M. (1995). Storytelling out of school: Undocumented college residency, race, and reaction. *Hastings Constitutional Law Quarterly, 22,* 1019–1086.

17. Passel, J. S. (2006). *The size and characteristics of the unauthorized migration population in the U.S.: Estimates based on the March 2005 Current Population Survey.* Washington, DC: Pew Hispanic Center.

18. Fortuny, K., Capps, R., & Passel, J. S. (2007). *The characteristics of unauthorized immigrants in California, Los Angeles County, and the United States.* Washington, DC: The Urban Institute.

19. Passel, J. S. (2001). *Demographic information relating to H.R. 1918, The Student Adjustment Act.* Washington, DC: The Urban Institute.

20. Passel, J. S. (2003). *Further demographic information relating to the DREAM Act.* Washington, DC: The Urban Institute.

21. Freedberg, L. (2006). Personal perspective: College for all Californians? *San Francisco Chronicle,* January 30.

22. Strayhorn, C. K. (2006). *Special report: Undocumented immigrants in Texas: A financial analysis of the impact to the state budget and economy.* Austin, TX: Office of the Texas State Comptroller.

23. Gonzales, R. G. (2007). *Wasted talent and broken dreams: The lost potential of undocumented students.* Washington, DC: Immigration Policy Center.

24. Garza, C. L. (2006). Immigrant students seek path to a dream. *Houston Chronicle,* April 6.

25. Massachusetts Taxpayers Foundation. (2006). *Massachusetts public colleges would gain millions of dollars from undocumented immigrants.* Boston, MA: Author.

26. Connolly, K. A. (2005). In search of the American dream: An examination of undocumented students, in-state tuition, and the Dream Act. *The Catholic University Law Review, 55,* 193–225.

27. Gonzales, 2007.

28. Fortuny, Capps, & Passel, 2007.

29.   U.S. Census Bureau. (2002). *The big payoff: Educational attainment and synthetic estimates of work-life earnings (No. P23–210)*. Washington, DC: Author.

30.   Bureau of Labor Statistics, (2007, August). *Spotlight on statistics: Back to school.* Accessed from http://www.bls.gov/spotlight/2007/back_to_school/data.htm#table1

31.   Borjas, G. J. (2000). *Issues in the economics of immigration*. Chicago: University of Chicago Press.; Lowell, B. L., & Suro, R. (2002). *How many undocumented: The numbers behind the U.S.-Mexico migration talks*. Washington, DC: Pew Hispanic Center; Martin, P. (2002). *Guest workers: New solution, new problem?* Washington, DC: Pew Hispanic Center.

32.   Rothman, E. S., & Espenshade, T. J. (1992). Fiscal impacts of immigration to the United States. *Population Index, 58*(3), 381–415.

33.   Powers, M. G., Kraly, E. P., & Seltzer, W. (2004). IRCA: Lessons of the last U.S. legalization program. Washington, DC: Migration Policy Institute.

34.   Papademetriou, D. G. (2005). *The global struggle with illegal migration: No end in sight*. Washington, DC: Migration Policy Institute.

35.   Arango, J., & Jachimowicz, M. (2005). *Regularizing immigrants in Spain: A new approach*. Washington, DC: Migration Policy Institute.

36.   Papademetriou, D. G. (2005). *The "regularization" option in managing illegal migration more effectively: A comparative perspective*. Washington, DC: Migration Policy Institute.

37.   U.S. Census Bureau, 2006 American Community Survey; C05002. Place of Birth by Citizenship Status; and C05005. Year of Entry by Citizenship Status; using American FactFinder®; <http://factfinder.census.gov/>; (accessed: 16 January 2008).

38.   U.S. Census Bureau (1999). Historical census statistics on the foreign-born population of the United States: 1850–1990. Population Division Working Paper No. 29.

PART ONE

High School Students

1 <u>PENELOPE</u>

"I know for a fact my success is because of my relentless determination."

AT the beginning of her senior year in high school, Penelope came to terms with the harsh reality that her undocumented status would affect her future educational opportunities in the United States. It had been only a year since she first learned about her legal status. Now on the cusp of graduating from high school with an excellent academic record, participation in numerous extracurricular activities, and a recipient of myriad academic and community service awards, she is worried about not being able to afford college, "I want to go to a university, but it is too expensive. They don't offer a lot of benefits for people with my status. Financially, I can't do it. I can't." Penelope's worry about paying for college is a common experience for many students as they near high school graduation. The financial concern for undocumented students is even more intense because they are not eligible for any form of federal financial aid. Undocumented students must figure out on their own how to pay for college.

At a time when most students are deciding where to apply to college, Penelope was worrying about whether it would even be an option for her. She had always dreamed of going to college, but all of a sudden she felt that her educational opportunities were limited. When I interviewed Penelope, she vividly described the feelings of hopelessness she experienced just a few months earlier when she tried to map out her college options:

> At the beginning of the year, I was just freaking out. I was thinking, "Oh, my god, I am not going to get good educational opportunities!"

Compared to my friends' opportunities, my opportunities were pretty low. It's just hard. I think it can be done, but it's just hard."

Even though she had always planned to attend college, Penelope was now dealing with the reality of her being undocumented as a major barrier. Although she knows getting to college will be an uphill battle, she is ready for the challenge; she is ambitious, goal-oriented, and determined not to give up on her dream.

Penelope has overcome many hardships in her personal life to get where she is today. She was only nine years old when she came to the United States with her family. She had a very difficult childhood and was raised by her mother when her parents separated when she was very young. Sadly, Penelope did not see her mother much because she worked long hours to support her and her two sisters, "My mom would work all the time. She would never have time for us." Although her mother was a strong role model for Penelope, her demanding work schedule did not allow her to spend quality time with her daughters. Penelope's parents reconciled several years later, and shortly after, they decided to immigrate to the United States. With only a few possessions, Penelope's family made the long, difficult journey to the North in search of a better life.

The economic hardships her family faced after immigrating to the United States were trying. As is the case for many immigrants, finding a stable job and affordable housing was challenging. This instability forced Penelope's family to move around frequently when she was young. The constant moves had a significant impact on her education because every time her family moved to a new place, she had to change schools. She attended three different elementary schools, making it hard to develop a sense of stability and belonging. She explains, "It was really hard for me to adjust to the environment. It was difficult making friends. I hardly ever had friends. It was even more difficult because of the language." Despite moving from place to place and the difficulty of adjusting to new schools, Penelope still excelled academically, making the honor roll at each school she attended. From a very young age, Penelope already showed signs that, despite adversity, she was determined to succeed.

When Penelope first started school in the United States, she was placed in English-language development (ELD) classes with other recently arrived students who did not speak or understand English. Although she acknowledges that the ELD classes assisted her in learning English, she felt that being in ELD isolated her from the social scene at her school and held her back intellectually. Penelope was placed in ELD classes from elementary school until high school. In fact, when Penelope started ninth grade, she could not believe she had been placed in the ELD track again, which was keeping her from taking the necessary college-prep courses. After lengthy negotiations with the school, Penelope was allowed to enroll in her first Advanced Placement (AP) course. She was very excited to finally break free of the ELD track and start working toward her goal of going to college. She reflects on taking her first advanced-level course:

> I remember my first AP class, AP biology. I really remember that because when I got to high school I was still an ELD student. I never thought I would ever actually be with the smart people. I thought that the farthest I would go was into a regular class.

Taking an AP class "with the smart people" was a wonderful and life-changing experience for Penelope. For the very first time in her academic career, she felt that she was being challenged intellectually. After officially switching to the college-bound track, Penelope continued taking numerous academically rigorous courses throughout high school:

> AP biology was the first one. That was my sophomore year. Junior year I took U.S. history, English, Spanish, and calculus AB, and then in my twelfth-grade year I took government last semester, and right now I'm taking AP economics, AP Spanish lit, AP calculus BC. I think it was a challenge for me, not only as a student, but as a person. I thought, if I can do well, I can basically do anything. That was my main motivation for taking those classes.

Getting good grades in her AP classes gave Penelope a new sense of herself as a good student. With a new sense of confidence, Penelope continued working toward her goal of going to college.

As described earlier, one of the biggest challenges Penelope faces as an undocumented student is constantly seeing the sharp contrast between opportunities available to her and those available to her U.S.-born friends. She is very aware of the many doors that are closed to her because of her lack of legal status:

> As a student, I think you want to do all the things that your friends are doing, getting your driver's license, for example. They have the advantage of being able to work. The only job we can get after we graduate is going to be a really bad job like at a factory or something, while they will get all the benefits, like working at a bank or working somewhere that is going to help them in their career.

As she now plans for college, and compares her options to those of her U.S. citizen friends, she describes applying for college as a very different process for her, "You don't have a choice. It's what you can afford, not what you want." Penelope feels that her lack of legal status in this country takes away her freedom to choose her educational path. Whereas her classmates get to choose what college they want to go to, she feels that she will not have a choice. She also knows that her friends will be able to get financial assistance to attend any college; for her, college will be decided based on her ability to pay the full cost of tuition out of her own pocket. In recognizing all the disadvantages she faces as a result of not being a U.S. citizen, Penelope tries not to despair, and instead constantly looks for sources of hope and inspiration to keep her from giving up.

Penelope credits her parents for helping her to stay positive and motivated to keep moving forward in pursuing her education. Their stories of personal struggle growing up in poverty without the option of going to school inspire her, "They tell me about their childhood and how it was hard for them to get to where they are now. It has given me a reason to continue with school." Her parents constantly remind her that she needs to follow a better career than they have working as manual laborers in factories:

> They have always motivated us to do better than they are doing. They're basically working class. Now I see that I don't want to be that. I want

something better for myself and my future. They didn't go very far in school. They finished elementary school and some middle school.

Penelope also sees education as a pathway to financial stability. With a college degree, she feels she will not have to worry constantly about money as her family has done most of her life, "My family has been struggling financially. I just want to have a stable life. I don't want to be rich or anything, but I want things to be taken care of, have my own house."

Another source of inspiration and drive for Penelope are other undocumented students who have gone to college. She personally knows a number of such students who were able to pay their way through college and get their degree, but are now unable to use their degree to get a job, "I do know some who have graduated from college. They already have their bachelor's degree, but they can't work because they don't have their permits. But they have their education. I don't think that's fair." These students' not being able to use their college degrees in the workforce is sad, but she draws strength from the hope that her story will be different. Penelope has also learned from these students how to be resourceful in finding scholarships to assist with the cost of school to remain hopeful:

> They have been very helpful. They have given me some ideas on how to get money from private scholarships. They have given me advice on my career . . . how I should always follow what I want to do. They have influenced me in the way that you can actually achieve your dreams. They have taught me to never give up.

When asked about whether she worried that she may not be able to get a job after finishing college just like the undocumented college graduates she knows, she responds candidly with an uncanny sense of optimism, "It doesn't, because even though they can't work, they don't give up on their dreams. They are still fighting." Similarly, Penelope is not giving up on her dream of earning a college degree and actively surrounds herself with people whose stories affirm her drive and determination.

In high school, Penelope got very involved in extracurricular activities on the advice of a good friend:

> She actually motivated me to get involved in a lot of academics in my school. She made it seem like it was possible, and it was. She gave me a lot of motivation. So I did participate in a lot of academic clubs, like the math club, the science club, the social science club, speech and debate, academic decathlon.

Not only did Penelope participate in these clubs, but she also assumed various leadership positions:

> I am the president for the speech and debate and the social science clubs. I am also the secretary for the science club. I am a member of Academic Decathlon, and I participated in the super quiz, which was televised. Being in the clubs was great.

As a result of her academic excellence and extracurricular involvement, Penelope has received many awards and recognitions:

> I've been on the honor roll and received achievement awards. The honor roll has been pretty much every year of high school. For the achievement award, you have to pretty much maintain an A or B average. I also got an award because of my grades and community service. I worked at the hospital, and I also volunteered at a school tutoring kids during the weekends. I work with middle school kids, elementary school, and high school kids—it's from 10 am until 3 pm on Saturdays—and for the hospital volunteering, I go three times a week. If it's during the weekdays, I do two hours. If it's on a weekend, I do four hours.

Penelope credits her strong determination as an important factor in her school success, "I know for a fact my success is because of my relentless determination." She also credits her optimism, "What makes the difference is that I have a positive attitude and most others don't."

Academics and extracurricular activities were not the only commitments Penelope had to balance in high school. Since middle school, she has had various responsibilities at home, which include taking care of her younger sister:

> I have to help my parents with my little sister. I take care of my little sister every day. It takes a lot of my time after school from 3:00 pm until 5:00 or 6:00 pm, or until they get home. I also have other responsibilities. I have to clean the house, the kitchen, the living room, my room, do the dishes, vacuum, make the beds. I actually don't start doing my homework until 7:00 pm.

Unlike most high school students who can dedicate all their free time to school and activities, Penelope had to set aside time to assist with household chores.

Penelope has overcome many barriers in her path to educational success. A significant aspect of her life that has motivated her is growing up in an impoverished neighborhood. She said that most children in her neighborhood "gave up" on school and life. Although this sounds like an environment that might foster feelings of hopelessness, Penelope had a different reaction. Instead, being in this environment strengthened her desire to not end up like most kids she had gone to school with:

> Where I live, most of the kids give up. They give up on their education. I don't want to think that it is something that is impossible for me. I want to think positive. I really want to continue with what I am doing in school.

She also wants to avoid the fate of getting pregnant at an early age, which happens to many young girls in her neighborhood, including her sister, "In our community a lot of the girls get pregnant or drop out. My sister got pregnant at an early age." Her sister's pregnancy left a lasting impression on her and further motivated her in school, "The one thing that has really put my mind into going to college was my sister getting pregnant. I saw how hard it was for her to go to school."

Reflecting on Penelope's amazing high school record of accomplishment, her strength and perseverance became even more obvious when she shared with me that her mother was diagnosed with cancer when she was in 10th grade, "My mom got cancer my tenth-grade year. It was really hard for me. I had never gone through that stage of knowing that someone in my family could die." Although Penelope has encountered many events in her life that could have easily altered her dreams of going to college, she never gave up on working toward her goals. Despite the many educational hindrances of being undocumented, Penelope always finds people and activities that keep her motivated and moving forward.

Penelope wants to become a pediatrician. She understands that, financially, medical school is not a viable option for her, so she has a backup plan, "Right now I know I'm not going to have money for medical school, so I need to be smart about it. I'm choosing nursing first, before I apply to med school." Penelope continues to plan her educational and career goals around her undocumented status. Until her status is legalized, she will not be able to pursue and accomplish her educational goals.

2 JAIME

"It's almost like I am tied down to the ground with a ball and chain because I don't have citizenship."

ALWAYS on the move while growing up, Jaime is now looking for a permanent place he can call home. He hopes that one day, with citizenship, it will be the United States. Jaime was four years old when his family came to the United States in search of better opportunities. Although not the first or last move Jaime would experience, this one would be the most significant in changing the course of his life. His move to the United States made him feel like he was getting closer to home, but when he arrived he realized he was still very far away.

Jaime has endured frequent moves throughout his childhood. In Mexico, his father was a truck driver, an occupation that required his family to move around a lot. The constant moves made it hard for Jaime to feel an attachment to one place he called home, "My family moved from place to place. We always felt like we never had a sense of security." His father's job also forced him to be gone for long periods during Jaime's childhood:

> My father is a hardworking man. He works as a truck driver, so he makes a decent living, but sometimes he neglected the family because . . . he had to be away. He traveled and he missed out on my growing up and being with the family.

Despite his father's absence, Jaime recognizes the many sacrifices his father made to support the family, "I missed out on my father and that hurts, but somebody had to work. He sacrificed himself so I could have an education, and I don't want his hard work and sacrifice to go to waste." In the end, Jaime feels his father has given him an extraordinary opportunity to get an education, which serves as constant motivation to succeed in school.

Jaime described his elementary school years as difficult both at home and at school. At home, he struggled to deal with the attention his younger sister received when she was born, "It was hard because when my sister was born, my father started giving her more attention. You could say that I felt some jealousy over that." At school, Jaime struggled to fit in, "I always got along with other students, but I always felt isolated." As early as elementary school, Jaime was trying to find a place where he felt comfortable and accepted. Despite his social difficulties in school, he recalls getting very good grades in elementary school, "I always maintained As and Bs. I don't remember ever getting a C."

Middle school was the first time in Jaime's life that his family did not move, allowing him to start and finish at the same school. This stability allowed Jaime the opportunity to become involved in extracurricular activities, and this is when his passion for school and music prevailed. Jaime participated in the band for two years, "I played the percussion instruments. My second year, I was the first chair for the percussion." Jaime flourished academically during this time and was on the academic honor roll for two semesters. He was placed in honors courses and was identified for the Gifted and Talented Education (GATE) program in eighth grade. Although he was very proud of his academic accomplishments during middle school, he sometimes felt ambivalent about embracing his new identity as a good student because he was called a "nerd":

> It was tough being called the nerd in middle school, but I realize that that is who I needed to be. I realize I needed to be a hardworking student because I wanted this for myself, and if I didn't do it for myself, nobody else would.

Middle school was also when Jaime began to connect with teachers who helped him succeed in school. Jaime credits one of his middle school science teachers as having a strong influence on him, saying, "She helped me understand that you can find things through research. I think that is how I developed some of the research skills that I really love." This teacher introduced him to a passion he would continue to pursue in his educational endeavors. For the first time in his life, Jaime was starting to develop an attachment to one specific place, his school.

Just as Jaime was beginning to establish roots at school, he learned that his family would be moving once again. Shortly before starting high school, Jaime's family moved to a different state. Jaime was very distraught that he would have to start all over again. As with all of his moves, he knew he was going to be the new kid who would have to make new friends. Although he had a new group of friends by the end of high school, he was still considered the "new kid" on the block:

> I've tried to have fun with some of the people that I met, but some of them wouldn't accept me. It was hard. Even after four years, some people still don't accept me because I'm still considered to be a new person. I didn't grow up with most of them, so it's still hard.

Although socially Jaime had a hard time establishing strong connections with his new friends, he continued to pursue his passion for music and excelled academically in high school. He was in the band for four years, serving as first chair of the percussion section. He was also involved in running the summer band camp: "Whenever August came around, I always went to band camp. I helped run this year's band camp." In addition to the school band, Jaime plays in a local community band, "I play in two community bands and they're very entertaining. We perform in different venues. We go to shows. There are people of all ages in the band." Jaime is also in a rock band. In fact, his musical talent was recognized by his peers, who voted him "band boy" for a student recognition website:

> I think they saw my devotion. Some people tell me that I work hard and that I never stop playing. And I think that's very true. Music is my passion. It's what drives me. It's like a little motor inside of me trying to get me to go from one place to another. That is how I feel about music. It can make you feel happy and it certainly makes me feel happy.

It became clear when talking with Jaime that music gave him a sense of stability and belonging, often allowing him to connect with others as he moved from place to place while growing up in search of a place to call home.

At the time of the interview, Jaime was only a few weeks away from his high school graduation. Academically, he had done exceptionally well in high school, graduating with above a 4.0 grade point average (GPA) and ranked 6th in his class of 300. At the senior awards ceremony he had recently attended, he received four different awards in recognition of his academic achievements. In addition to taking rigorous classes in high school, Jaime took courses at the local community college his senior year:

> I took two courses my first semester and three courses the second semester. I had a personal desire to experience some of the college classes. It's a great thing to do. I recommend it to anyone who is in their last year of high school, if you have the time, because you need a lot of time. It's a good experience.

Despite his commitment to his high school courses and band activities, Jaime excelled in his community college classes:

> In one of the classes I was at the top of the class. It was a computer class. I felt really impressed that a high school student could step up to the plate and stay there with the college kids, because the college kids have more time to do the work than a high school student who is involved in the music program and who has his own AP classes to attend to, but has the ability to actually study in that community college and get the highest grade. So I am just impressed with my own ability.

Like most students in this study, Jaime balanced family responsibilities with school and his extracurricular activities. At home, Jaime takes care of his younger sister when his older sister and parents are at work. He explains, "It's hard because my mom, dad, and my sister are sometimes always out of the house so I have to take care of her." During the summers he, "had to stay home and babysit." Although Jaime sometimes endures the stresses of balancing all of his commitments, he thinks that the people around him admire him for being able to maintain involvement in all his activities. He says, "I am admired right now in this place in time because I have managed to balance my life with all my classes in school and at the community college and through the music program and all the other activities that I'm involved in."

One of the biggest disappointments Jaime has faced in being undocumented is not being able to follow his dream of joining the U.S. military. He explains the extreme disappointment he experienced his junior year in high school when he was actively pursuing this goal, "At the end of my junior year, I was trying to get into one of the military schools, but I realize that without citizenship it is impossible." Jaime was extremely disappointed when he realized he would not be able to attend the Naval Academy at Annapolis. He had already received a very high score on the military school entrance exams, which won him acclaim:

> I had such a high rank in that test that the administrator decided to tell the principal about my high score. The administrator told me that I could easily enroll in any military school of this nation, so I tried to get accepted. I wanted to go to Annapolis because, after you go there, you can easily be accepted into the Marine Corps.

As Jaime reflects on his missed opportunity to join the military, he explains how he feels being undocumented:

> It's almost like I am tied down to the ground with a ball and chain because I don't have citizenship. If I did have citizenship, I would be able to do some things that I can't do now, like my plans to go to Annapolis. I know I would have succeeded there because I have determination.

After having been rejected from military schools due to his undocumented status, Jamie decided to apply to college and was accepted to two excellent public universities. Unfortunately, Jaime's legal status has kept him from being able to call the United States home and serving in the U.S. military.

Jamie believes that he and his undocumented friends are driven to do well in school as a result of their legal status, "We realize that if we don't work, we aren't going to succeed, especially because we don't have citizenship, so it is our goal to work hard and make sure that we succeed in life." His ambition is demonstrated by his view on how students should approach their learning and success:

> It's like in the workforce you want to be the manager or the highest person in a store, but there's another person who can be the manager, so you work harder to try to show your leadership abilities and you do any special tasks that are given to you. And you try to accomplish them because you want to succeed. You want to get that manager position in that store. That similar thinking goes in the classroom with other students.

Reflecting on the challenges he has encountered as an undocumented student, Jamie states, "It's almost like you don't have a say. You don't have a right to vote. If I had the opportunity to vote, I would certainly use it. It's a privilege, so why would I waste it?" Despite his challenges and need for help and support, Jaime prefers to keep his legal status a secret:

> I choose not to tell people about my status because I don't want them to know that I don't have any papers or I'm not a citizen because it certainly feels like I am being isolated, and that is what I don't want.

Jaime made this decision after his father was arrested for being undocumented and was forced to sell his house:

> My dad decided to sell the house because he was arrested for not having citizenship. But after they checked his tax records, they decided to let him go because he is an honest worker. But I felt afraid because now [that] they know we are here and they might come and deport us.

Fortunately, Jaime's father was not deported, but the reality of knowing he could be thrown out of a country to which he has now grown very attached forces him to live in constant fear.

Jamie has decided that he wants to become a music professor and performer. He says, "After consideration, I have decided to remain with the music and try to become a music professor, maybe become a professional musician, work in the industry for movies." He realizes, however, if he wants to get an advanced degree, he will probably have to pay for it on his own, "I know in order to get that Ph.D., I'm not going to get any money from the government, and I'm going to have to do it all on my own."

Jaime has taken all the necessary steps toward being able to call the United States home, but his undocumented status keeps him from fully realizing that dream. Although he has established strong roots in this country through his many wonderful educational accomplishments, he is still on the margins of society and is reminded of that every day. Only by legalizing his status in this country will Jaime finally be able to call the United States home.

3 JERONIMO

"It's like someone giving you a car, but not putting any gas in it."

JERONIMO's story is one of an amazing young man with a Mexican heritage but an American identity. Although he values and embraces his American identity, Jeronimo is constantly reminded of his lack of legal status, which prevents him from being considered a true "American." Born in Mexico, Jeronimo came to the United States when he was a year old and has lived in the United States all of his life. Even though he considers himself "American," the U.S. government does not, which he feels is a missed opportunity for himself and this country:

> There are a lot of people that just because they don't have the opportunities, waste their talents, waste their abilities, that could be beneficial to any country. I believe that if a student like myself was raised in this country, grew up here, studied in America, learned by American teachers, I feel American. I mean, I cannot feel Mexican when I don't know anything about Mexico. I learned about America, I studied their government, I studied their culture, I know their culture. . . . I feel like an American student, and I think that labeling someone just because [of] where they were born rather than what they know and what they feel, I don't think it's right.

Jeronimo feels that through his efforts and success in school, he has not wasted any opportunities offered to him in this country. He believes he has been a productive member of American society and that he should be rewarded, not punished.

As American as Jeronimo considers himself, he is surprised he is so frequently made to feel on the margins of society as a result of his status.

The negative sentiment most Americans feel toward immigrants due to media influences is a part of Jeronimo's daily existence. Unknowingly, people around him often voice their negative feelings toward undocumented immigrants without realizing he is one. This occurrence, which Jeronimo has experienced on numerous occasions, makes him feel rejected:

> When they don't know your status, and they feel free to talk about their beliefs, feel free to talk about what they think, what they feel about the issue, they say things like, "Oh, what are they doing here? They should all go back to where they came from." You know, you feel discriminated against. As someone who was raised American, how am I supposed to say anything to that? There's not much you can say.

Jeronimo feels very silenced in these types of situations. He believes society is sending him a message that he is not American, which is confusing for someone with a strong American identity.

Jeronimo is reminded of his legal status almost daily. In high school, when he was starting to plan for college, he felt as if doors were opening up for other students and closing on him because he was undocumented:

> Second semester all these great opportunities opened up for people, and you suddenly feel like your door is closed [because of] being undocumented. They come in showing the PowerPoints about federal aid and Cal Grants and it says, "Undocumented students cannot apply," and you feel horrible. Everyone has this great opportunity, and you feel like you don't have anything.

It is interesting that the more Jeronimo plans for college and his future, the more he feels closed off from those educational opportunities he seeks. His efforts to accomplish something no one in his family has done before—earn a college degree—actually highlight the extent of his limitations. This was a very disappointing time in Jeronimo's life.

Like most students profiled in this book, Jeronimo always saw himself going to college in the future. Even though his parents are not highly educated (his father went to middle school, and his mother finished one year of high school), they were strong advocates of school and college:

I never saw myself not going to college. We were always told that in order to have a good life and in order to succeed, we need to keep going with our education, and that always was imprinted in my head. I never saw myself not following my education.

Sadly, following his dream has lead Jeronimo to ongoing disappointment. He says, "In my French class, they would take the top students on trips to France during the summer, and I knew I couldn't go because I can't get a passport and it was just horrible. You feel restricted from so many things." He also wanted to join the Reserve Officers' Training Corps (ROTC) in high school, but was unable to because U.S. citizenship is required to participate.

There's the ROTC at school, I know I couldn't get involved in that because it was required to take numerous trips to Air Force bases, but you can't get into an Air Force base without any formal ID, and obviously I couldn't get an ID.

In addition to missed educational opportunities, Jeronimo has been forced to decline important employment opportunities because of his inability to produce needed legal documentation. On one occasion, he was offered a job as an assistant manager at a computer store, but he didn't take it because he knew he would need to produce a Social Security card:

I was offered an assistant manager job because I know about computers and I've taken computer courses and they know I know all the programs, so they wanted me to start an assistant manager's job at $9 an hour, but, of course, I can't because, you know, I have no documents.

Jeronimo concluded his reflections about the various ways in which his legal status has restricted him by vividly describing how he feels being undocumented, "Restricting undocumented students from federal aid is like someone giving you a car, but not putting any gas in it. I mean, you can't go anywhere. You have it, but you can't use it." Even though he often feels like a "car without gas," he continues to work hard in school,

"I always tried to be at the top. I would feel like a personal failure if someone ever got, like, outstanding student over me."

At the time of the interview, Jeronimo was only a few days away from graduating from high school with a 4.02 GPA, and he ranked 17th in a graduating class of 500. As such, he has received numerous awards for his various academic accomplishments in high school:

> I received a lot of academic awards, like the academic stars for the letterman's jacket. I received best musician and I also received the Outstanding Musician from Bank of America award. I also completed the Phoenix Program, which is the honors all the way through high school, and I got into the Honor Guard for top 10 in the junior class, and when I was on the golf team, I received the Outstanding Sophomore Golf or Outstanding Junior Golf or Outstanding Senior Golf.

Jeronimo's academic achievements in high school are no surprise since he started excelling in school at a very young age. In elementary school, he received many academic awards. He recalls, "I remember I used to win a lot of Student of the Month, Outstanding Student, and all that stuff. Also, I was involved in music and I would always get Outstanding Musician awards." He recalls becoming fluent in English fairly quickly, compared to other kids, "I remember the bilingual classes. . . . I remember me being bright. I was like the second person next to another girl that became fluent speakers of English."

In middle school, Jeronimo joined the GATE program and again received numerous academic awards. He says, "I received a math trophy, a math award, musician awards, numerous outstanding awards, outstanding student awards, academic awards, a 4.0 GPA award." He also continued his participation in the school band as well as in sports and academic enrichment programs. In band he was first chair for the trumpet and baritones, and he was captain of the soccer team.

In high school, Jeronimo continued to expand his band participation and got involved in other extracurricular activities:

> I was involved again in the band, the jazz band, the symphonic band, the marching band, the pep band. I was also on the golf team for three

years. I was in the Alive in Christ Club—it's a Christian club at school—the Economics Club. I was also involved in the AP program.

He was vice president of the Alive in Christ Club and captain of the golf team his senior year. In band, he was first chair and was also chosen to be drum major. In addition to his band participation, Jeronimo volunteered at a local community theater as an usher.

Even with all of his amazing accomplishments, Jeronimo could not apply to four-year universities after high school because he could not afford the cost without assistance. Since Jeronimo does not qualify for financial aid, he began planning to attend community college, since it was the most affordable option:

> I would go to a community college, and as soon as things are fixed, because we already have the process going, . . . I would eventually go into a university. I mean, there's nothing wrong with going to a community college and then transferring, and that's what I was planning. I said, "Okay, I'm going to have to go to a community college and then go into a university studying music or business or government."

Going to a community college is a very typical pathway to higher education for many undocumented students because it is affordable.

Although Jeronimo has always been interested in law and politics, he fears that his status may prevent him from following a career in those areas, "Well, I've always been interested in politics, actually, or law, maybe [be] a lawyer. I've always been interested in history, government, but there are a lot of complications with me joining United States politics obviously." In the future, Jeronimo has ambitious plans to pursue a degree in business. He says, "I want to get my degree in business and keep my music on the side. I want to one day be head of a business." For Jeronimo to be given the opportunity to accomplish his goals, he needs to become legalized.

4 LILIA

"I want a chance to work in an office with air conditioning
rather than in the fields under the hot sun."

LILIA came to the United States when she was 10 years old. She recalls fond memories of her life in Mexico before arriving here. Lilia remembers being very close to her family, especially her aunts and grandparents on her mother's side. She recalls, "My mom's family was always there. They always provided everything I needed." In fact, Lilia was left in their care for a year before joining her parents and brother here in the United States. Her father immigrated by himself four years earlier, and her mother and brother came one year before she arrived.

Unlike the other students included in this section, Lilia came to the United States at an older age and thus remembers her childhood in Mexico very vividly. She constantly draws comparisons between her experiences growing up in Mexico and her life in the United States. Her dual frame of reference profoundly affects the way she views her opportunities here. Drawing these comparisons motivates her to take full advantage of all the educational opportunities available to her. She reflects on the numerous resources available in the United States compared to her native Mexico:

> I don't take things for granted. I remember when I first came here in the fifth grade I got a free lunch at school. Back in Mexico, you have to buy your own stuff because nothing is for free. I had friends in Mexico that would faint in school because they didn't have anything to eat. It's really that bad. Some people can't go to school because they have to work. One of my school friends in Mexico had to start working when

> he was twelve, so he kept repeating the same grade and his mom was illiterate. Another friend one time came to school without doing her homework, and the teacher asked her why, and she said it was because they didn't have any light. It is those drastic things that make you realize you're lucky just to have a roof over your head.

Having a roof over her head, however, is not the only privilege Lilia acknowledged about living in the United States. Throughout my interview with her, the Mexico-U.S. comparisons kept emerging as a perspective Lilia draws on to remind herself to keep moving forward.

Lilia was enrolled in fifth grade when she first arrived; she had completed first through fourth grades in Mexico. When she started doing work in her class, she quickly realized that the education she got in Mexico gave her an advantage over her American classmates:

> It was a small school, it was sort of a rural area. I went from first to fourth grade with the same people, so I knew all of them. Most of my teachers were very good. I learned a lot. When I came here, I was even more advanced than the American kids, mostly in math.

Lilia received high recognition for her academic performance in Mexico. She says, "I was a very good student back then. They have something sort of like the Standardized Testing and Reporting (STAR) testing there. They test statewide, and depending on your score, you got an award, so I got an award for that."

Even though Lilia was more academically advanced than her classmates, she still had a very difficult time adjusting to the American school system. The hardest part of her adjustment was the language barrier. She was initially placed in an English-only class and felt completely lost because she could not understand anything her teacher was saying:

> It was a really hard year for me. It was mostly the language barrier. In the fifth grade, they don't have bilingual classes, and my teacher only spoke English. Sometimes for two weeks straight I was really lost in class. I would try to get information from the people who sat next to me, but they really didn't know how to explain things to me, so I was really stressed out about that. I told my mom and she said there was

nothing she could do because there was no bilingual education in that grade.

It was not until Lilia spoke with her neighbor that she realized she could ask to be placed in a class with a Spanish-speaking teacher who could accommodate her language needs:

> One of my neighbors that was in my same grade told me that his teacher spoke Spanish, so even though it wasn't bilingual education, I could still ask him things. So they switched me to his class. He let me turn in assignments in Spanish and sometimes he would just teach me things on the side.

This teacher spoke to Lilia in Spanish and allowed her to turn in assignments in her native language as needed, which helped her feel more grounded in the academic work. Slowly, with her teacher's assistance, she started making great strides in school.

When Lilia transitioned to middle school, she was enrolled in ELD classes. Unlike her elementary school, which did not have any type of bilingual courses for its non-English-speaking students, her junior high did offer such classes. Once placed in the ELD classes, she began to realize just how much English she had learned in such a short time compared to her classmates:

> So I got into an ELD class, and it was just helping students learn English. My science and English teachers were both bilingual. They would explain in English and in Spanish. Each year they do a test to see how fluent you are, and barely a month had passed by and they tested me. And that was only the second time I had taken the test, and it said that I was fluent already, and so I had to go to a regular English class.

Within a month's time, Lilia was close to fluent and ready to join mainstream classes. Even more impressive, after Lilia moved to the regular English-language courses, she distinguished herself as a "top student" by the end of her first year:

It was really weird, because by the end of the year, I was the top student in that class. It was only my first year, and I was already getting high scores. Then my English teacher asked me if I had been recommended for honors classes. In seventh grade, I was enrolled in honors classes.

Lilia was very proud of her quick transition to the honors classes after not understanding a word of English just two years earlier. She recalls, "It was great. At first it didn't really sink in, but after a while I thought, wow, in two years I made a huge step from nothing in ELD to the honors classes." In addition to her quick transition into academically rigorous courses, Lilia was tested and admitted into the GATE program, "In seventh grade they tested me and I passed." Lilia's quick ascent into the honors program attests to her desire to succeed, something she hopes will eventually earn her citizenship.

Lilia was in 12th grade at the time of the interview. According to her account, the highlight of her experience in high school was interning for a state senator during the previous summer, an opportunity offered to her through her school. Knowing she would never have had this opportunity in Mexico, she quickly signed up. Her experience working in a senator's office made her realize how different the legislator's work was compared to her undocumented Mexican immigrant father:

> I saw how easy it was for someone who graduated from college, their work. Then I would look at my dad. He didn't get a good education. He is undocumented. I see his hands all rough from the work that he does. He is in construction. He's always sweating. His face and his arms are always all sunburned in the summer. When I was at the capitol it was in the middle of July, but people were working in buildings with air conditioning. Their jobs seemed so easy to me. I felt like I could do this any time. They can go out for lunch any time. I want a chance to work in an office with air conditioning rather than in the fields under the hot sun. I realized that education opens a lot of doors for you.

As usual, Lilia saw the sharp contrast between being Mexican and being American as well as being a citizen rather than being undocumented. Lilia sees the many opportunities available to American citizens, and that makes her work hard in school because she feels education is her pathway to legalization.

After hearing Lilia compare her dad to the workers at the senator's office, it is no surprise that she identifies her parents as a strong source of support. She says, "They always push me to do well in school. Since I was little, my parents would push me a lot. My dad always tells me to look at him and the work he does so I can do better." Even though Lilia's parents have low levels of education, they are strong advocates of higher education. Her father has a middle school education, and her mother attended a vocational high school, but was unable to complete her program due to family circumstances.

Lilia learned about her undocumented status during ninth grade when she first started thinking about college. She recalls, "I know there are options, but even if there are colleges, the list of where I can go is going to be limited." Despite learning about her undocumented status early in her high school career, she has still done exceptionally well. During her senior year, when I interviewed her, she had a 3.7 GPA and was ranked 15th out of a class of over 300. She continues to take honors and AP courses, including AP Spanish and AP U.S. history. In fact, she received a very prestigious award for maintaining above a 3.5 GPA as well as making a perfect score on the California High School Exit Exam (CAHSEE), "For CAHSEE, if you get a 380 or above, you get an award. I got a perfect score."

Lilia has also been very involved in extracurricular activities in high school. Through an academic outreach program, she has been involved in several community service activities, saying, "They had us clean. We went to a nearby city and we just cleaned an alley. It took a long time. We just cleaned and picked up things." Lilia is also involved in drama, "Recently for drama we did this Dr. Seuss day. We put on a skit and read to elementary school kids." Lilia enjoys being involved in activities that enhance her community.

Lilia has faced many of the same challenges as other undocumented students at this level. Once again, by comparing her situation with that of her friends, she sees the many advantages of being a U.S. citizen. She cannot obtain a license, as her friends can, on turning 16. Lilia says, "I can't drive because I can't get a permit because I don't have a Social

Security number." Like Jaime, she had to give up a highly coveted job because she could not produce the needed Social Security card:

> Last summer I applied for this job at a bank. They only picked one student out of the entire class, and they only offered it to the English honors class. I had to interview and I had to write an essay. I went through all of that and I got the job. I was really excited about the job. I had a really flexible schedule, and it looks really good on a resume to work at a bank at such a young age. The pay was really good, too. During my second day of training and orientation, they called me in and told me that they might not be able to keep me, so I lost my job because of that.

Lilia wants to continue with her education so she can take care of her family and set a good example for her younger siblings:

> I want to help my parents because I doubt my mom can work, so they are going to need money. And my brother, I don't know if he will eventually be here legally, but if he needs to go to school, I could help him with the money.

She also sees her educational advancement as the pathway to citizenship. Cherishing every opportunity available to her in the United States, Lilia knows that becoming a citizen will broaden her options in the future. Thus, she remains hopeful that her legalization will happen soon.

PART TWO

Community College
Students

5 DANIELLA

"I've always had a passion for community service."

DANIELLA always saw herself as different from the children she grew up with. Unlike her friends who were enjoying their youth, she grew up quickly and assumed adult responsibilities in her family at a very young age:

> I was worrying about how are we going to pay for rent, how am I going to go to school. My parents are not there, my parents are not supportive, my parents don't understand, and besides, they were worrying about other things.

Daniella grew up in an economically depressed neighborhood of Los Angeles after arriving in the United States at the age of four. Her mother worked in a factory, and her father worked in a restaurant. As the oldest child in her family, it was her responsibility to take care of her younger siblings when her parents were at work. Perhaps it was these responsibilities that helped her develop amazing leadership skills that came in handy in school later in her life. As early as elementary school, Daniella was admired for her exceptional leadership:

> I don't know if it's a talent or an ability, but I guess I always had this leadership aspect. I was always very helpful. I always loved to help people. When I was in elementary [school], growing up, my teachers loved me. I was always on top of my work, I was always chosen to be the leader of something. I was chosen to give a speech for *Cinco de Mayo*. I was chosen to recite a poem just because people saw, I guess, that I was able to do it. I have spoken up when I needed to or when I had to, and I was

sure that I needed to stand up for what I believe in. But, yeah, I guess in that aspect I was admired for my leadership.

Taking on numerous leadership roles at school no doubt contributed to Daniella's lifelong passion for community service. It is very important for Daniella to help out in her community in any way she can. She explains that this commitment started in high school, when she took a community planning class:

> It opened my eyes to what was going on with my community and how could I help. I mean, I've always had a passion for community service. I always see things that other people haven't really taken a chance to look at. I could never ignore things. People my age are not usually worrying about poverty, or why people can't go to school, those sort of things. I can't ignore that because that's in front of me, and I always feel an obligation or a responsibility to do something.

Daniella feels that her ability to see inequalities in our society obligates her to do something to help improve conditions for those less fortunate. She believes this is a part of her American spirit of giving. It is not surprising that Daniella has received monetary recognition and awards for her commitment to community service in the form of scholarships and awards. "Right out of high school, I got eight scholarships," she says. In total, Daniella received $10,000 worth of scholarship money when she graduated from high school, most of which was the direct result of her community service efforts.

Daniella feels good about the service recognition she has received. From it, she has developed a renewed sense of confidence and optimism:

> When I got my first scholarship, I was like, "Oh, my God! I actually got a scholarship." I never thought in my life I was going to be getting money from people for writing a paper, and when I got my first check, I was like, "Oh, my God! I can't believe I got my first check." But I did. The more I started applying, the more I realized, "You know what? This is possible." That's how I'm paying my way through college, with little scholarships.

Three days before our interview, Daniella had received a $2,000 scholarship from a national health care provider. This was an achievement she was very proud to report. In addition to scholarship money, Daniella has received recognition from the California State Senate for her community service work. Community service was not her only interest during high school; she was also involved in various extracurricular activities. She played on the tennis team, was in the Spanish club, and participated in the color guard as a freshman. She was also a part of the California Scholarship Federation (CSF).

Daniella also balanced her academics with working in high school. She worked 16 hours during the weekends and additional hours during school breaks and vacations to start saving for college. In fact, Daniella began looking for a job when she realized that she would have to pay for college on her own. She knew she could not count on her parents for any financial support.

Daniella's experience was very different from most students in this book who have very supportive families. Her parents did not support her educational pursuits and, instead, told her she could not afford college. She explains:

> My parents were not supportive, and every time I told them that I wanted to go to college, they'd say, "No, because we don't have the money and we can't pay for it." So that kind of brought me down and I started thinking, "Oh, man, I got to find a way to save money because my parents are not going to help me. I've got to do it somehow." So in 10th grade, I went looking for a job, and one of my friends got me a job, and I'm still working there . . .

Daniella's relationship with her parents has always been contentious. When she was younger, she resented her parents and blamed them for her legal situation:

> I was going through problems with them just because I would blame them a lot for my situation as far as being an undocumented student, especially when I applied for certain things and was rejected. I know it was not the right thing, but I blamed my parents for bringing me here, and I wasn't very happy.

When I interviewed Daniella, she was a first-year community college student. She could not afford to go directly to a four-year university so she started at the more affordable junior college:

> I felt that going to community college would just give me a little bit more time to . . . raise more money, to find more resources, and hopefully, by the time I graduated from community college, I would just need to raise a little more money to pay for the university.

She decided to attend a college that is far from her home because she had heard that it helps undocumented students. In fact, the school she attends has scholarships specifically for undocumented students. For that reason, she finds her daily three-hour commute on public transportation well worth it. An unexpected challenge for Daniella, however, is the ethnic makeup of her school. She is now attending a predominantly White college, which is very different from the working-class Latino community she grew up in. Growing up, she had very little contact with other groups, so her new college environment was an adjustment:

> I felt culture shock when I got there. I always thought that culture shock was when a White person went to another neighborhood, and I never thought about it like a Latino going to a White neighborhood or a different neighborhood. I was feeling defensive, I was feeling like I had to guard what I was, my identity, what I stand for. I felt like somebody was trying to take it away from me.

Once again, Daniella is very different from most of the students around her. She continues to have adult worries beyond her age, unlike her White classmates who can focus on school. As Daniella makes her way through college, her undocumented status continues to be frustrating. She says, "You want to show them so much of what you have to offer, and they don't really want to hear it. I just don't want to stop educating myself because of my legal situation."

Daniella does acknowledge a few key individuals in her life who have had a positive impact on her education. She fondly remembers a middle school teacher who made her feel important and encouraged her to forge ahead despite other teachers who treated her with disdain. Even though she was a straight-A student, she says, "The teachers were not very supportive. They never really talked about Latino kids going into college or never really expected them to go to college." In junior high, she finally met a teacher who truly cared about her:

> He was just the best teacher I ever had. He was not like everybody else. He was this Latino teacher that came from an area just like the one I came from, but had graduated from a big university, had gotten his degree.

He was not only a role model, he also set high expectations to motivate her. She recalls, "He always told me, 'You know, I'm going to be there for your high school graduation, and then when you go to college, I'm going to be there,' and I guess that's something that I needed."

As we near the end of the interview, Daniella reflects on the irrational and insensitive view most Americans have about undocumented youth, "How could they do that to somebody that has been living in this country for most all their life, and all of a sudden they're just going to say, 'You don't belong here'?" She does not understand why she constantly has to live on the margins of American society as an undocumented student when she makes such a great effort to be productive and to give to her community whenever she can.

Despite her sense of rejection from American society and its refusal to acknowledge her contributions and commitment to civic participation, Daniella cannot even imagine a different future from where she grew up, trying to make a difference in other people's lives. As such, she hopes to work as a teacher or for a nonprofit organization. Her passion for service continues to grow even stronger in college:

> It's always been very rewarding for me when I do community service. I feel that, yes, I'm giving back. I feel that, even though I was not given a lot, I feel there's other people that don't have enough; they're in a worse situation than I'm in. I feel that if I'm aware of what's going on, even if other people choose to ignore what's going on in their community or just choose not to help, I choose to help.

Daniella is determined to work hard and achieve success in her education, career, and life. As she grows older, she still treads a path very different from that of most other kids in her neighborhood:

> A lot of my friends got pregnant at an early age, have not continued with school, and most of my family members also didn't finish high school. A lot of my cousins got pregnant, and people always point at you and say, "You're next. You're next." But for me, I was like, "No, I'm not going to. I have dreams, I have goals, and I'm going to achieve them. Even if it takes me more than the time that it's supposed to, I will." And up until this point, I'm still doing and keeping up with what I have told myself that I needed to do.

For all of her amazing efforts to contribute, Daniella hopes one day to be rewarded by American society and given a pathway to citizenship.

6 ISABEL

"They say you can accomplish whatever you want or set your mind to, but they don't say that it's just for some."

OVERCOMING adversity and managing to stay focused on a goal is one of Isabel's strengths. She came to the United States at the age of four, and when she arrived, she lived in a very rough neighborhood with gangs and violence. She has had to compromise in many ways just to survive her childhood. In fact, she had to become friends with many of the individuals who scared her the most just to get by. Although she was friends with many gang members growing up, she never actually joined a gang and was able to opt out of their activities. She explains:

> The gangs were pretty heavy, so, yeah, I used to hang around with people that belonged to gangs and stuff like that, but was not part of them. I mean, you could be friends, but you don't have to do the same things they do. You have the option of, you know, say like, "Yeah, I'm with you guys, but I have other things to do."

From a very early age, Isabel found ways to protect herself from the numerous negative influences in her neighborhood and remain focused on school. Somehow, she has always managed to keep her eye on the prize.

As she progressed through the education system, school became Isabel's sanctuary, a place that was safe and gave her a sense of purpose. In junior high, she would take classes during her semester break just to keep busy. She recalls, "I would go to intersession and take extra classes and stuff like that, and they would take us to field trips and expose us to different environments." Although taking classes during the intersession was perceived as "nerdy," she felt that the time away from her neighborhood removed her from the dangerous gang activity. At the end of junior high school, Isabel's hard work and dedication paid off when she received an award for having one of the highest GPAs in her class, which gave her great pride.

High school was a bit more difficult for Isabel, in part because of the cruel disappointment of finding out she was undocumented. She did not learn of her lack of legal status until she applied for her first job at the age of 13. She explains how the discovery led her to the conclusion that her legal status in this country would limit her educational options:

> This guy was like, "Oh, we'll help you fill out the application." Then I see the letters "SS" and I'm like, "What's SS?" They're like, "Oh, Social Security number." "What's that?" They say, "Oh, I'm sure you have one. Just ask your mom." And I went home, I asked my mom, "Mom, what's a social security?" and she says, "Oh, well, it's this number that they give to citizens," and I'm like, "Do I have one?" She's like, "No, you don't." I'm like, "So that means I can't work?" She says, "No, I'm afraid not," and I'm like, "Oh, okay." It didn't hit me back then how serious that would end up being later on. That was the first time that it opened my eyes to the fact that I was limited. In school, they say you can accomplish whatever you want or set your mind to, but they don't say that it's just for some.

Later, in high school, when Isabel began planning for college, was when the full extent of her limitations occurred to her. Even though she had known years earlier about her status, she continued working hard in school with the belief that she would be rewarded for high academic achievement. As her search for college persisted, so did her realization that what her mom had disclosed to her years ago would continue to haunt her dreams of going to college. She says:

> It was right around the end of my junior year, when you start applying for colleges and looking for financial aid for your senior year. That's where like the whole world fell down you could say for me for awhile, because this whole time, from 9th grade to my junior year, I worked

hard in classes. I wasn't a straight-A student, but I was good. I had good grades and everything, and I worked hard; I did do well with my extracurricular activities. And then when I go to the financial aid office and the career office, they're like, "Oh, well, you can't work because you don't have papers. We have places that are hiring, but you can't work because you don't have a social." So, alright, whatever, it's not a big deal right now because I'm in high school. So I went to the financial aid to get money for school, they're like, "Oh, well, just fill in the facts." And they helped me out and they're like, "Oh, you have to put your Social Security." And I'm like, "I don't have one." "Oh." Pretty much the same thing. That's where it came back, what my mom told me a long time ago and like, "Well, if you don't have one, you don't qualify." And I'm like . . . so this whole time I studied, I did all I could do and then, just like that, you close the door on me, and I was like, "Wow! That hit me." That got me depressed for awhile. It did. Senior year I wasn't the same because now I'm like, "Okay, now what am I going to do?"

Isabel did everything she was told to do: study hard, participate in extracurricular activities, and get good grades. She had done very well in high school and was in the honors program. She consistently volunteered at a local community organization, a senior center, and her church. At graduation, she received several awards for her excellent academic record. In addition, she had taken courses at the local community college during the intersession to earn college credit. She recalls, "I would go to the college, Trade Tech, and I would take classes over there. That's where I took my psychology and history classes over there." Isabel always went above and beyond the requirements to ensure her success.

Sadly, after all that hard work doing exactly what she was told, the rug was pulled out from under her when she realized that she could not go any further. The messages Isabel received about her contributions were devastating. As Isabel notes, "If you're going to reject a person just because of their citizenship, you will be missing out on so many people that are gifted and contribute so much." Even though Isabel felt like a wall was in front of her, she refused to give up, a theme that runs through many biographies of the undocumented students I interviewed. In fact, Isabel still plans to start at the community college and transfer to her dream school, New York University:

My plans were to come to the community college for two years and then transfer to NYU because I was accepted. So I'm like, "Alright, then I'll do that. So at least I have a hope and that's all I can care for right now." For financial aid I'm like, "Alright, well that's a problem, so instead of dwelling on the problem, I'll just find a solution." So then I'm like, "Okay, I'll look into scholarships." In high school I was in a mentor program that awarded me a $500 scholarship, so that helped me out for, like, the first two semesters. I just started looking into other scholarships to help me along the way, but then tuition went up and something that would have taken two years, it's taking me forever right now. But, I mean, I'm still here, I haven't given up, and I know it's a long process, but I'll get through it.

Despite her best efforts, Isabel continues to struggle to pay for school. Her high school activities helped her secure a few scholarships from organizations that she volunteered for, but she still cannot get all the funds she needs. Sometimes she does not even have enough money to pay for her monthly $54 bus pass.

Instead of becoming discouraged by her financial situation, Isabel is resourceful and finds ways to stitch together money to pay for college. In the process, she remains confident that she will get through it and accomplish her goal of getting her bachelor's degree from NYU. In light of her daily struggles, Isabel's drive and dedication are remarkable, while her work ethic is equally impressive:

In order to really get through it you have to want it badly, to say, "Okay, you know what? I'm passing this class. I'm going to do my best and stay committed to it." And you know how sometimes you can study for a test, but there's like those extra things you could do to prepare you even better or get that extra knowledge, I knew I could do it, but I wouldn't bother and that would make a difference from an A to a B, and I'm like, "Okay . . ." Like the last good grades I got was last summer. I took Art 72 and I took cinema and I got As for both of them. And I'm like, "I haven't got As for a long time," because my self-esteem has been down, my determination hasn't been all it could be, and my drive hasn't been there. I mean, I'm still here struggling, but I notice that you have to want it badly to really get over it . . . not get over, but accomplish it.

In the future, Isabel would like to major in psychology and work as a counseling professional.

In many ways, school and political activism fuel Isabel's determination and optimism. She draws strength from actively working to change the conditions that are responsible for her marginal state. During college, she became very involved with a local immigrant rights organization:

> I'm really active there. Right now we're planning and organizing a rally and marches. We're going to go to Sacramento to lobby, and then we're going to go to Arizona for a four hundred-student conference, and we have workshops along the way, too, so it's really busy.

Isabel also came to the following realization about getting involved:

> After a while I just got tired of complaining about my situation, so I'm like "Okay, you've been complaining for so long, so what can you do about it?" And that's how I started getting involved. I'm like, "Don't just be the one that complains. If you're going to complain, do something about it, then you can complain." So that's how I got involved. I was tired of just being in that situation, so now I could do something about it, have some sort of control over it."

Since she was a child, Isabel has always been active in changing her social circumstances and continues to do so as an adult.

Like many of the students I interviewed, one of the main reasons Isabel was motivated to do well in school and pursue higher education is to set an example for her younger siblings:

> As the oldest, I want not only more for myself, but also for my siblings. I want them to know this is not just the only life, that there's more out there. There's more in the world that you could go and accomplish. So, yeah, I just want to set a positive example for them and know that it's hard, but not impossible.

Even though Isabel faces many obstacles in her own pursuit of higher education, her dedication to supporting her siblings education is remarkable:

I see my parents and I see the hard work that they do and how they break their back and whatnot and I'm like, "Whatever they're doing, I could at least do something better for them." That and my siblings, as the oldest I feel that it is my responsibility to set a good example. And it has worked because now my sister graduated from high school, she's going to Trade Tech, to study culinary arts, and my brother, he's going to graduate this upcoming year from high school and, hopefully, I'm going to help him out so he can go to college, too. You know, help him out little by little, and the littlest ones, my two little ones, they know they're going to go to school because they know the struggle I'm going through and my other brothers are going through, and they know they have to go to school. And one of them was like, "I'll be a teacher, a doctor, or maybe the president." "You go, girl. You could be whatever you want." So it's not in vain.

Although Isabel realizes that her legal status holds her back, she stays very optimistic that her time will come. She knows she just needs to be patient, stay focused on the goal, and keep moving forward:

It's a challenge not being able to fulfill all that you are capable of because you're being constantly held back, and you see that the doors are closing on you when you're trying to move forward. But every time that one door closes, there's always another one along the way that will open, so you just have to be looking for it and keep your eye on what you're going to do.

For now, Isabel is keeping her eye on the door to citizenship in hopes that it will open for her very soon.

7 LUCILA

"I don't belong here because I don't have my papers,
so it's kind of like I'm in limbo."

LUCILA is driven by her passion to help people in need. Although she has made numerous significant contributions to American society, she is still denied the privileges of an American citizen. The fact that she is denied access to opportunities only makes her determination to succeed stronger. Despite societal rejection, Lucila embraces her American identity and dreams of someday being recognized as a full-fledged U.S. citizen.

In line with Lucila's desire to be a citizen, her biggest disappointment as an undocumented student was not being able to join the U.S military:

> I wanted to join the military. I wanted to go into the National Guard, and I didn't get accepted. I did all my training. I started getting fit because I wanted to make sure that when I got to boot camp I was going to be able to do things. I showed my recruiter all the paperwork that I had, and he said, "We're going to be able to get you in." I was like, "Cool, I really want to do this." I remember I had to starve myself the week before because I was like five pounds overweight, and I got there and I was there at 3:00 in the morning ready to go, ready to sign in, ready to do my paperwork, and I remember the guy telling me, "This isn't enough paperwork." I was like, "What do you mean this isn't enough paperwork? The recruiter said this isn't enough." He said, "No, you're missing more stuff from INS [Immigration and Naturalization Service]."

For Lucila, military service would help to assert her American identity. When I asked her how her interest in the military developed, she responded:

> I don't belong in Mexico and I've always been here. This is the only place I know, but after that [being denied for military service], it was kind of like, "Where do I belong?" I don't belong there, because if I go back there, I'm a little White girl who can't really speak Spanish very well and then not here because I don't belong here because I don't have my papers, so it's kind of like I'm in limbo.

Like most of the students I interviewed, a significant part of Lucila's life has been her community involvement. She began her volunteer activities in middle school and has continued to be active ever since:

> I volunteered at a convalescent home. I started doing that, like, in middle school, where my mom used to work. I would go in and help with activities with the old folks and help them do bingo and I did that, and then right after high school, I started volunteering for the Red Cross.

Lucila had taken a semester off before starting community college to volunteer for the Red Cross to go help victims of Hurricane Katrina. This experience most certainly speaks to her empathy and extensive civic engagement. When I asked her to share how she made such a big decision to go to Louisiana, she recalls:

> I was sitting one day with my mom and we were watching everything that was happening during the disaster and stuff, and I remember my mom saying, "You know, somebody needs to go and help them. And I was like, "You know what? I'm going to go down and see if I can answer phones or something and help locally." She said, "Okay," and my dad went and dropped me off. It was about two weeks before I was going to turn eighteen. I got there and they asked me, "Well, do you want to work here, or do you want to be deployed to the area to help?" And I said, "Well, if I can help, anywhere you guys want to put me." She was like, "Well, you can fill out a deployment application." So I filled it out. They called me a couple of days later to tell me, "Look, here's your

mission. Call this number. Your plane leaves this day," and I celebrated my eighteenth birthday out there.

According to Lucila, making the decision to help was easy, and with her parents' assistance and support, it happened very quickly. Helping with the relief efforts was a life-changing experience for Lucila. Just as she learned from the other volunteers who had come from all over the country, she also educated them about undocumented immigrant students, which was a very affirming feeling:

> There were people from all over the country who came to volunteer, and there were people who had never seen different cultures. I remember being very open with them when I got there and telling them, "You know, I'm only seventeen. I'll be eighteen in a couple of days, and, yeah, I am an illegal immigrant." And everybody was kind of in shock. Like, I remember seeing some people from like Missouri and North Dakota just looking at me like, "You're what? You're an immigrant?" And I remember the first thing, like, them looking at me, like, and I'm like, "I'm just a college student trying to get by." And I remember these people just having a new image of what an immigrant was like, and I think that was the biggest impact that I've ever had because I remember telling these people, "Look, we don't come here to take your money. I'm just trying to get an education and succeed in life." And I remember them being in shock that I was so young and out there willing to do stuff.

Aside from her numerous and extensive volunteer activities, Lucila has excelled in school throughout her educational career. Although she acknowledges her achievements, she also notes that her academic success has been the product of both teachers who supported her and those who discouraged her. In both instances, these experiences fueled her motivation and desire to do well in school.

Lucila first described an elementary school teacher who was very supportive and encouraging:

> I had one teacher who made the biggest impact in my life. I think out of even middle school and high school, that one teacher I still talk to.

She was the one person I sent an invitation to when I graduated from high school.

According to Lucila, Mrs. S was also a great role model, "She was the greatest teacher I ever had. She always told me I could do whatever I wanted, always emphasized that there is no level that a women cannot reach." As a result of Mrs. S's influence, Lucila was placed in the Gifted and Talented Education (GATE) program in fourth grade. Thus, this teacher had a major impact on Lucila's educational trajectory.

While Mrs. S was an excellent role model and mentor for Lucila, her seventh-grade math teacher, Mr. R, was the exact opposite. In fact, he openly questioned her academic abilities:

> I remember when I was doing speech and debate and I was practicing for my competition, I asked him, "You know, this might take a little bit of time inside one of your classes; can I take that time?" And he said, "Well, you can go ahead and take all the time that you want." He was like, "I don't even know why you're competing." Because there was a girl who was in eighth grade and I was in seventh, he goes, "She's going to win anyways, so I don't understand why you're going to go and practice, so go ahead and take all the time you want." And I remember taking that and being so angry and going back and writing my speech and doing all this stuff, and I remember at the very last competition, when I was at the state competition, he showed up with his wife, and I just remember laughing because I had the highest grade in his math class. And I was a seventh grader who did a speech and I won state championship and I beat out seniors in high school; him ending up at my competition, I just thought it was great.

Lucila relished proving her teacher who doubted her wrong. Instead of allowing his comments about her ability to win the speech competition to discourage her, she used his negative attitude to motivate herself to work harder and win. The fact that this educator discouraged her fueled her to excel even more.

Similarly, in high school, Lucila had a negative experience with her academic counselor, who doubted her ability to go to college. She relates:

> In high school, I had a counselor. It was the same counselor my sister had, and this counselor told my sister that she wasn't going to be able to do it. My sister told her she wanted to be a lawyer, and she told her, "Oh, no, your people are better off doing housework." She put her down, so I didn't even want to go to my counselor and ask her for help. I just felt so discriminated . . . it's like, "I already know what you think of us. Why even go in there? You already labeled me. There's already a label on my forehead thinking that I should be a housekeeper, so why go in and ask you what classes I should take? You're already going to tell me what classes to take, to take home economics.

Lucila graduated from high school with a 3.8 GPA, and while in high school she participated in mock trial, winning several competitions. In addition to the few extracurricular activities she participated in, Lucila worked. In 10th grade she worked 20 hours per week as a secretary at a financial advisory firm. The office was just down the street from her school, so it was very convenient. She also worked at a fast food restaurant for several months and at a grocery store for two years during high school. Reflecting on the balance between school and work, Lucila recalls:

> I wasn't really allowed to go out and party and stuff because my parents weren't big on us going to parties, or at least not with me because I'm the baby and I'm the girl. So they emphasized more school, and my dad wasn't really happy when I got my job because he always used to tell me that as soon as we saw money, we were going to forget about school. But I showed him that I could do work and school, and I was really proud of myself because I didn't have to rely so much on them because I had a job. I was able to pay for senior prom, homecoming, all those things, and buy myself my dress and stuff that I couldn't have gotten if I had not been working.

Even though her parents discouraged her from working for fear it would take away from her study time, Lucila insisted. She liked working for pay because it gave her a strong sense of independence.

Now in college, Lucila continues to work, but for different reasons—to pay her tuition. Without access to financial aid, Lucila has had to take time off to work to save money for her college expenses. At the time of the interview, she had been working for five months in the pediatrics wing of a local hospital, which has led her to consider a career in social work in the future:

> I love kids, I love working with kids. I'm looking into social work, probation officer, or even running my own foster home. I think that would be one of the biggest things. I would love to be able to just take in kids and take care of them.

Lucila articulates her frustration in doing everything right, everything that one is supposed to do to become a contributing member of society, and having that not be enough, "It's kind of hard because it's like I'm doing all these things . . . like I've done volunteer work, I've gone with the Red Cross, I'm willing to go out there." Lucila continues to wait for this country to finally recognize her for her diligence in "doing everything right."

8 PAULINA

"I catch the bus at 5:15 am; I literally sleep with my clothes on."

PAULINA shared a painful memory from her childhood early in our conversation that framed her struggles as an undocumented student. Growing up, Paulina was intellectually curious and looked for any excuse to go to her local library. In fifth grade, she had to do a report that required a trip to the library. That visit forever changed her positive feelings about her intellectual sanctuary:

> In fifth grade I had to do a report on Pocahontas. I selected to take out my own library card, and they said only with your mom's signature. I was like, "Okay, I will bring my mom." Then they asked my mom for ID. She said, "Well, I have my passport." They said, "No, that's not good enough." I remember I was so upset. I was like, "I just want one book. I will bring it back." You know, kids don't understand.

Rejection and disappointment came at an early age for Paulina. As early as elementary school, it was made very clear that her lack of legal status was going to hinder her ability to pursue her intellectual interests and educational goals.

Paulina came to the United States from Mexico when she was nine years old. She is the eldest of four siblings and the only one not born in the United States. Paulina started her education in Mexico, which she felt had prepared her well for school in America. In Mexico, she attended a Catholic school with very rigorous course work. She recalls, "When I came here, I remember I was supposed to be in third grade, but they pushed me up to fourth grade just because I was a little more advanced. It's because it was really rigorous over there."

Paulina always enjoyed school. As she explains, she was part of the "nerd crowd." Her classmates often called her "schoolgirl" because, "I talked to teachers a lot. I would always do my work. Yeah, I guess I did kiss up once in awhile." She never missed school and received awards for perfect attendance in both elementary and middle school.

In middle school, her history teacher had a major influence on her:

> I would always talk to him about what I wanted to do. He would just be like, "Yeah, anything you want to do you can do it. You just have to set your mind to it." I just felt like in a dreamy state every time I was with him. I was like, yeah, I can.

In contrast to her experience at the library, Paulina's teacher made her feel as if anything was possible. Having a supportive teacher helped to alleviate some of the earlier disappointment and rejection she felt that day at the public library. As she would soon learn, however, not all teachers would be supportive of her educational pursuits; throughout her education, she has had many who were negative and discouraging.

In high school, she had teachers question her academic abilities. Paulina felt that many teachers had negative assumptions about her because of her ethnicity. She also felt isolated in her advanced courses because she was one of the only Latinas in those classes. She often felt unwelcomed in her AP courses because, she says:

> They were like, "What are you doing here?" but joking. Nobody said it in a serious tone. But sometimes it did feel like that. It was from the people that I hung out with or socialized with. I was the only one who was actually interested in classes. I was the one who used to think that research is fun. I was the only one. It was really upsetting. That's why I felt like I couldn't do a lot of what I wanted to do.

It certainly did not help matters any that the school Paulina attended had a lot of racial-ethnic tensions among Whites, Hispanics, and African Americans that affected classroom and social activities.

Even though Paulina's AP courses were isolating at times, she enjoyed the academic rigor and intellectual challenge. For the first time, Paulina was inspired to go to college when she started taking AP courses:

> I think that's when my goal to pursue a college education started. It was just so fascinating because the teachers were so passionate about what they were teaching, and I was like, "Whoa!" They made it seem interesting, and I would actually enjoy going to the classes. And although it was more work than the normal classes, the work we did get was interesting. I mean we were doing the romantics and British poets, and I was like, "Oh, my god! This is fascinating! I love these poets!"

The racial-ethnic climate of her school led Paulina to participate in extracurricular activities that helped her explore her Latina identity. She joined a club, called "Amigos," and decided to take on a leadership role in the club, serving as vice president. Paulina also participated in choir for two years until she started working part time after school. In 11th grade, she took a job at a local video store working 25 hours a week. Unfortunately, she resigned after four months because her boss sexually harassed her. The trauma of the event even caused her to fail a class that semester, permanently tarnishing her high school academic record.

Now in college, Paulina's struggles continue. She cannot drive to school because she is not eligible to obtain a driver's license and must rely on public transportation. Sometimes she cannot schedule her classes during times that correspond to the bus schedule, presenting another challenge to her education. She explains her daily school schedule taking the bus:

> I catch the bus at 5:15 am; I literally sleep with my clothes on so I can just roll out of bed. I get to school at 6:15 am. Then I go to class at 6:30 am, and then I have three classes. I just stay there all day; I don't come back until 9:30 pm when I get out of my literature classes. In the middle I have nothing, but since my house is so far away for me to take the bus, I would rather not do that. So I have to pack everything for the day. I have to take my lunch and all the books that I might possibly need. It's really hard.

Paulina tries to study as much as she can at school because studying at home on the weekends can be difficult due to all the noise and commotion of the neighborhood and her family. She says, "They are fighting over the phone, over each other's things, or whatever. Outside, all the kids and people are playing loud music, people are yelling and screaming. There's always something. It's just really hard to concentrate."

Currently, Paulina is enrolled in the honors program at her community college. She joined after finding out about it from her friend and realizing that it would give her the academic challenge she desired. When she first started taking classes in community college, she thought they were too easy:

> I felt like junior college was high school part two. I wasn't being challenged. Then a friend of mine whom I had met in one of my classes told me about the honors track. I said, "What is so good about it? He's like, "It's just like a lot of more rigorous work. It's not just one piece of paper and then you're done." And I was like, "Really?" So I went and checked it out. It was work, work, work. So I applied for it.

As is the case for most undocumented students, paying for college is always a hardship. Says Paulina, "I think intellectually and academically I am just as good as anybody else. In some cases I think I'm better. It's just financial. Everything is so much harder." Her inability to get financial assistance in college has required her to work long hours to pay her tuition. During her first year in college, she worked at her parish's elementary school as an office assistant. The demanding schedule of commuting, working long hours, and being in the honors program took a toll on her academic performance, and her grades suffered. "It was just so tiring," she relates. In desperation, she asked her family for financial assistance. Luckily, her whole family has rallied around her to help her pay for school:

> My dad pays most of it, but I have a big set of cousins. They all pitch in and there are a lot of them. So they will help me buy books. One of them works at Staples, so he tries to get me my school supplies. I applied a couple of semesters for school scholarships that don't require citizenship and I've gotten some. But it's mainly my dad. Then I've asked my cousins to help pay for books and supplies. One will buy the textbooks, and others will buy something else.

Fortunately for Paulina, her family is vesting in her education, and the investment has already begun to pay off as she has been accepted and willattend one of the most selective public universities in the United States.

As echoed in many of the stories in this book, one of the hardest parts of being an undocumented person in this country is living with the constant fear that the government will deport you. Paulina expressed to me her daily fear of being discovered by authorities:

> I think I am always afraid. I am walking down the street or wherever, and I am completely aware of myself to make sure that I am not doing anything I am not supposed to. Being responsible for everything that I do, making sure I am not doing anything at all. I'm just afraid. I'm afraid that one day someone will say, "You're not supposed to be here. Let's take you out." I'm constantly afraid . . .

Paulina is not the only one who lives in constant fear. All of the undocumented students I interviewed mentioned always living in the shadows and feeling vulnerable.

Paulina has a strong sense of purpose for her future. She wants to follow her passion and teach literature at the high school level and, eventually, at the college level. She says, "I want to teach with the same passion that I was taught with. That is my goal. I feel that that is my purpose." She knows that to teach in college, she has to get a Ph.D. and lights up just thinking about the possibility, "I can't wait to be called a doctor, too! I can't wait till I get to the really hard-core research part of my career. I am so looking forward to that in graduate school."

At the end of our interview, she highlights her optimism and competitiveness as traits that have helped her excel in the past and given her the strength to persevere, "My optimism . . . without that I would not have done anything. Seriously, I would have given up a long time ago." Paulina has earned her membership in American society by the many contributions she has made to her community and looks forward to her rewards in the future.

PART THREE

University Students

9 ANGELICA

"I think I will do something big, I just need a chance."

ANGELICA describes her undocumented status as a "metaphorical wheelchair" by explaining, "There are so many things I want to do and can't do because I am being held back from all my potential." For Angelica, a second-year college student with a long list of goals and aspirations, being undocumented is a frustrating and constraining obstacle. Since finding out about her legal status in ninth grade, Angelica has experienced a steady increase in the number of roadblocks in her path toward higher education.

Angelica came to the United States when she was three years old. She grew up in a one-bedroom apartment with her parents and her sister. She is the first member of her family to graduate from high school and go to college; her mother has a sixth-grade education, and her father finished the eighth grade. Her parents always supported her college aspirations, even if they did not actually know what was required to get there. Says Angelica:

> It was always a given that I was going to go to the university; they just didn't explain how I was going to pay for it, how I was going to get in, or anything else. They would say, "When you grow up, you're going to go to the university"; that was it.

Angelica internalized those messages and knew that one day she would go to college.

Angelica's drive wavered when she first learned she was undocumented. She felt that her prospects of going to college were ruined. She recalls, "I wasn't sure if I was even going to be able to go to college. I was really depressed because I was outstanding in school, but I can't go to college." The stress was overwhelming, and shortly after learning about her legal status, she was diagnosed with juvenile rheumatoid arthritis. Her doctor suggested that the stress she was experiencing might have triggered the onset of the disorder. Before then, Angelica had never missed a day of school. To make matters worse, when people asked what was wrong, she could not share her big secret with them:

> No one knew. None of my friends are undocumented, so that was even more stressful because there was no one I knew who I could tell. I felt that if I told anyone, who is going to understand me? My best friend and everyone I knew were born here. I have Asian friends, White friends, everything. How do I explain to them what that means?

Battling her new health condition, while at the same time digesting her reality of being undocumented was very trying for Angelica, and her school work started to suffer. Angelica had always been an excellent student in high school. She did well academically and had taken numerous advanced-level courses, including honors world history, honors chemistry, honors biology, and AP psychology. When her grades began to slip, her teachers started to worry about her. She relates, "I remember a teacher pulling me aside and asking me, 'What's going on with you? Why are you not doing your homework? What's going on; you're not this kind of student?'"

Nonetheless, the trauma had a permanent effect on Angelica. She described her experience in high school like a blur, "I felt like I was in a cloud all during high school." She could not shake the burden of being undocumented because of the damper it put on her college plans. By senior year, she slowly began to recover. As she says, "I was like okay, I can't be getting bad grades. I need to see what I am going to do with my life realistically." That is when she began to research her options and discovered AB540, the California law that allows undocumented California high school graduates to pay in-state tuition at public universities. With a newfound optimism, she enrolled in community college and, "that is when I started having hope again."

As soon as she enrolled in community college, the first thing Angelica did was join the honors program and start planning her transfer to a four-year university. As is the case for most undocumented students, the choice to start higher education at the community college was an economic one. According to Angelica, "I went to a community college first because I knew there was no way I was going to be able to pay for four years at a UC, and I didn't want to go to a state college just because my dream school was UCLA [University of California, Los Angeles]." So Angelica began taking all of the courses necessary to transfer while working 30 hours a week to pay her tuition. It was very difficult, but she was determined to succeed. She says:

> It was really, really hard. I don't remember getting much sleep. I transferred in two years, always working and going to school and getting really good grades. I was on the dean's list just getting as many A's as I could.

At the end of her two years in junior college, her hard work paid off when she received transfer acceptance letters from several highly selective public universities.

In addition to working and taking academically rigorous courses, Angelica has always found time for volunteer activities that help the community. She volunteered extensively in community college, but since transferring to a four-year university, she has not been able to volunteer as much:

> I was volunteering a lot in community college, like Easter Seals, the Jewish home for the aging. I volunteered in the middle school I went to, and I have done some volunteering at some high schools. Since it cost a lot more here, and I am not able to have the jobs I used to have, I am not working, so I am taking a lot more units so I could graduate early because I don't have enough money to pay for the next year.

Due to a lack of financial aid, Angelica has had to curtail her volunteer activities in college, which saddens her. She also does not receive any financial assistance from her school or her family and must pay for all her living and tuition expenses on her own.

Besides the insult of not being eligible for financial aid despite her excellent academic record, Angelica became demoralized in college by having to work a job for less than minimum wage. She recalls, "The first job was really depressing. I am, like, I shouldn't be doing this. I had all these dreams growing up, and washing dishes and mopping for eight hours and lifting heavy things, that wasn't my dream." Once again, Angelica felt like her undocumented status was constraining her ability to find a decent job where she was not doing hard manual labor for low pay. After all, she was already in college working toward her bachelor's degree.

Despite her lack of financial assistance, Angelica continues her academic excellence at her current university. She is enrolled in the honors program, is taking five classes, and maintains a 3.5 GPA. She also volunteers for a local nonprofit organization, participates in university recruitment activities to attract local high school students, and is on the fundraising committee for a student group that supports undocumented students.

Although her ultimate dream is to become a senator, for now, she wants to become a teacher, eventually working her way up to principal, and be actively involved in local politics. She loves the study of politics and looks forward to voting someday. She also plans to continue her education eventually. She says, "I want to earn a Ph.D., just because there are not many Hispanic women who do have one, and I just want to set the standard for other women so they can say, "She did it; I can do it, too.""

Despite the many setbacks she has faced as a result of her lack of legal status, Angelica remains optimistic about her future. According to her, "Despite everything, I think I'm destined for greatness, I think I will do something big; I just need a chance." Until Angelica is given that chance by American society, she will continue to feel as though she is stuck in a wheelchair, constrained from the many opportunities she needs to reach her full potential.

10 SASHA

"You'll never get an A in my class because you're a dirty Mexican."

CONFIDENT. Tenacious. These were my initial impressions of Sasha, a college sophomore, when I first met her. Her story is one of perseverance, seemingly endless optimism, and deep concern for the welfare of other undocumented students like her.

Sasha recalls a pleasant childhood. She was raised by her grandparents when her parents immigrated to the United States. When her parents were able to raise the money to pay for her trip, they sent for her to join them. She was six years old.

When Sasha first arrived in California, she found herself in the middle of a wave of anti-immigrant sentiment fueled by then-Governor Pete Wilson. Californians had just approved passage of Proposition 187, which forbade most forms of social services to immigrants:

> I got here at the time of Proposition 187. I remember all the anti-immigrant sentiment at my school. I was very confused. I didn't understand why people were angry. There would be demonstrations at my elementary school, and I didn't understand why they were yelling at me. Why they didn't want me to be here. I didn't see how I could harm them. I thought my parents were nice people, so why where they yelling at us? Why were they being so mean? I didn't understand the whole legal situation.

Despite the initial negative reception when she first arrived, Sasha dedicated herself to school and to learning English. Gradually, with each grade, her English improved and her academic accomplishments began to increase. In second grade, she received an award for most improved, and in third grade, she joined a program for academically advanced students. She recounts:

> The year after I arrived, I joined the magnet program. I really enjoyed it because the groups were smaller and because they really pushed your critical thinking. They created an environment that was very friendly and incited the students to learn.

In fourth grade, she won a spelling bee competition even though she had only been in the United States for two years. She relates, "I was really proud of it because I realize that English was my second language, and I thought it was so wonderful that for many students it was their first language and for me it was my second." Throughout her elementary school years, Sasha was also on the honor roll.

Elementary school was not without its challenges, however. When asked about influential teachers in her life, her response was unexpected:

> In third grade, I had a teacher that was actually incredibly mean and intolerant. She would discriminate against a lot of the students based on their ethnicity. She would pick on me a lot. She would tell me things like, "You'll never get an A in my class because you're a dirty Mexican," stuff like that. She would ask the students to raise their hands if they wanted to be president, and she would put my hand down and say, "You will never be president; you should focus on other things." But it was the best thing she could have done for me because it got me to the point where I decided that, if she wasn't going to give me that A, I was going to become the best student I could possibly be to say, "You know, I have the capacity, and my status in no way equates to my capacity." Thanks to her, we had the state department of education come down and conduct an IQ test because she said I was mentally challenged. It was a really good thing because that is what put me in the magnet program. It really gave me a lot of strength to continue and to not listen to individuals that were so close minded.

For Sasha, her racist elementary school teacher's doubts sparked the academic success that would continue through the present.

Unlike most of the students I interviewed, Sasha had two college-educated parents. They would encourage literacy and reading for pleasure when she was growing up. She says, "During the weekends, there was always a trip to the library, returning books, or to read books." Due to language and social barriers, however, her parents were not able to transfer the full benefit of their college education to their lives in the United States. Seeing her parents make the best of their situation to provide her with educational opportunities helped to motivate Sasha further to do well in school:

> Both of my parents have college degrees from Mexico. Despite having a college degree, my mother was a housekeeper, and my father worked at a lighting company. Seeing them utilize their college skills to make things work really motivated me to see that they are working hard and they are putting their pride aside. They are taking jobs that they are not used to, and, perhaps, I should work really hard because they are doing this for me.

In middle school, Sasha was bussed to another city because of overcrowding in her local school. She continued to be enrolled in the accelerated program. She recalls, "My junior high years were very tiresome because I had to wake up at five in the morning, and I would [go to] sleep at ten at night because I had a lot of homework. I was in a magnet program." Having to travel a long distance to school made it difficult for Sasha to become involved in after-school activities:

> It was really difficult to be part of any after-school activities because I was bussed. If I had any after-school activities, instead of coming home at five, I would end up coming home at seven, and my parents didn't really like that idea.

During her first eight years of schooling in the United States, Sasha was an outstanding student despite the difficulties she faced learning a new language and having teachers who were not always supportive. She lost some of that momentum, momentarily, at the end of eighth grade when she first learned that she was undocumented. Suddenly, pessimism began to set in and going to college seemed out of reach. She says:

Because of my situation, I knew that it would be very difficult to move beyond high school. I was very apathetic towards the end. I felt that even though I worked extremely hard, I would have to work twice as hard to go beyond high school.

As Sasha transitioned into high school, the extent of her limitations as an undocumented student became even clearer. She began to see how other highly talented students were being denied educational opportunities beyond high school because they were undocumented. She shared with me a story that she described as "an influential educational experience" about a talented undocumented student who was accepted into the most prestigious private university in the world:

> When I started high school, there was a student who had gotten accepted into Harvard. She had a full scholarship. They were even going to fly her from over there to come home for free at least twice a year. She had this great packet. And then she informed them that she was undocumented, and they took back the offer. That really shocked me. She was an honor roll student. She was the valedictorian. This girl had volunteered everywhere. She was so involved. Here you have an individual that worked so hard, and she wasn't allowed to continue. It was not fair. She wants to work hard and she wants to contribute, and they are not letting her. They are not giving her access. That really shocked me and it made me want to say, "You know what, I am going to work hard now, and maybe I won't get into that university, but I will get into a university and I will be actively involved, and I am going to contact different representatives, and I will make them aware of students like myself."

To make matters worse, Sasha's high school was not an environment that was particularly conducive to learning. She attended an overcrowded, predominantly Latino high school with more than 3,000 students. According to Sasha, "I remember the first week of school having to stand in class because there weren't enough chairs." Despite the challenges of attending an overcrowded high school and her deep disappointment about being undocumented, Sasha continued to do what she did best, be a good student. Many of her extracurricular activities focused on making her school a better place for students. She participated in the cheer squad, the Spanish club, and student government, where she was the student affairs officer. She says, "I liked it because I was able to work for my school. Improve it. I really enjoyed that. Also, I liked it because it was a good experience. It was a good way to attain leadership skills." She also took piano lessons, attended an intensive summer math program, and did volunteer work. She recalls, "I would go to different businesses or community organizations and I would translate for people that didn't speak English." Like almost all of the students I interviewed, Sasha balanced academically challenging courses, extracurricular activities, a job, and responsibilities at home. In addition to her extracurricular activities, AP and honors courses, and working about 20 hours a week, she helped to take care of her disabled brother who suffers from cerebral palsy.

Despite the major demands on her time, Sasha continued to excel in high school. She received a student-of-the-month award in 9th grade and again in 10th grade. She was also recognized for her student government involvement. She recounts, "When I was in student government and student affairs, they gave me a little recognition for really working hard. I really liked that. It was very gratifying to know that they thought that I was working hard."

When I interviewed Sasha, she was a sophomore in college. She explained to me that her experience as an undocumented student sparked an interest in studying government in college. She worked as an intern for a legislator for about eight months, which "allowed me to see what I can achieve. What I can aim for. It opened my eyes to a lot of other issues that undocumented students face. I am particularly interested in immigration and education." Her interest in government has also led her to become involved in voter registration efforts. She says:

> During the different elections, even though I can't vote, I helped to create awareness within my campus. I encouraged students to register to vote. We had a voter registration thing where we had different organizations register people to vote.

One of the major leadership roles she has assumed during college is being the founding president of a student organization that supports undocumented students on campus. When asked to elaborate on her duties as president, she modestly replies, "I never really think of it as president. I feel that it is a collective effort. We had to give the title to one of us, and we decided that it would be me. But we all work really hard."

Despite her dedication to school and her various extracurricular activities, Sasha's challenges as an undocumented student do not escape her. She works 30 hours a week and pays for her college expenses with her job earnings, help from her parents, and several scholarships. Sometimes, however, it's not enough. She has had to take a couple of semesters off because she could not afford to pay the tuition. When asked to elaborate on some of her challenges, she shares the following story:

> I guess another difficult aspect is just different internships and programs that I don't qualify for. I have had my counselor tell me, "Oh, my gosh, your GPA is great! You would love this program. And, look, you fulfill the requirements." So I've filled out the application, and I get a call that says, "Yes, but you forgot to mention this so I'm sorry, you don't qualify." I've missed out on a lot of opportunities because of my situation.

What makes it all the more difficult for Sasha is that she has grown up believing in the American ideal of meritocracy. She has come to believe that if you work hard enough, you will reap the rewards. She feels a sense of betrayal when she sees other less-deserving students having access to financial aid and other resources that she has worked very hard to qualify for but is being prevented from receiving. She says, "I know students that have terrible grades but they are still getting assistance and everything and I don't, even though I have good grades and I work hard."

What is so impressive about Sasha and most of the students I interviewed is their optimism and resourcefulness. Rather than resign herself to being locked out of internship opportunities, she flips the tone of her story by proclaiming:

> In spite of that, I really would like to say that I have made an effort to work beyond that and to say, "Well, if I can't be a part of that internship, I am going to find one that I can be a part of." I really want to do something. Even though things are difficult for a lot of us, we really do

make an effort to find ways to keep on learning, volunteer, and be a part of different events.

She even sees a silver lining in being undocumented:

> I guess some aspect I am happy for is that part of my situation has really made me appreciate my education. It makes me grateful for what I have. It incited a passion for government. It has allowed me to participate.

But for Sasha, being undocumented is more than being locked out of academic opportunities or lack of money to pay the tuition bill. It's also about living in constant fear:

> Being undocumented, you feel like you can't confide in people because there are people that will call the INS and tell them, you know, "This person shouldn't be here." I have that fear that maybe someone who doesn't like the fact that I am in college or the fact that I am here will do something. I have a fear that when my parents are driving on their way to work or going to church, or when we are going to the library, that they are going to stop us and say, "Go away, we don't want you here." I always have that sense of uncertainty.

Sometimes it's difficult for Sasha to imagine a brighter future when her fellow undocumented classmates graduate with a college degree but can't put their degree to use. In those moments, it's almost impossible to be optimistic. She says, "I know a couple of students who have graduated with degrees in biochemistry, government, and film. They have graduated and are working at a grocery store or in construction now." But for Sasha, quitting is not an option. She feels a deep obligation to be a role model for other struggling undocumented students. She needs to be strong for them. Most recently, she was inspired by a young woman who stood up during her university orientation and shared with the audience her story about being undocumented to help newly enrolled students feel they were not alone and that they could succeed at the university. Sasha was deeply moved by her bravery and seeks to follow her example:

> She had the strength to share her situation. I see her and she is involved. I see those students that are in high school or junior high

school, that are in my same situation, and it is my job to show them that it can be done.

Although she does not describe herself or her family as extremely religious, religion has helped her and her family cope with the hardships they have endured:

> We have our beliefs, and these principles really help guide us in difficult times. When my parents lost their jobs, for example, and during that whole thing with Proposition 187 in the early nineties, it helped us get through it because we decided to go along with the principles and teachings that taught forgiveness and compassion and stuff like that. I guess those principles helped us overcome difficult situations.

In the future, Sasha would like to be either a college professor or a lawyer. She wants to use her educational training to work on social justice issues. She explains, "I would love to work for an organization like Legal Aid. My ultimate goal is to utilize my education to improve communities that need assistance." As we near the conclusion of our interview, I ask Sasha to imagine that, instead of talking to me, she's talking to a group of state and federal legislators who are trying to figure out immigration reform legislation. This is what she would say to them:

> A lot of undocumented students embrace higher education. We just want an opportunity to show that we feel that this is our home. This is the only home we know. We are ready to contribute. We are ready to be a part of American society. We want the chance to be future doctors, police officers. We want that opportunity. We want to contribute, but we need your help. I need you to see how much a part of the United States we are, how much we identify as Americans because this is our home.

11 EDUARDO

"I'm restricted in joining clubs, participating in school events, taking on leadership roles . . . it's a bit damaging in the long run."

EDUARDO considers himself "just like everyone else," a typical American boy. He describes his childhood as ordinary and carefree, "My childhood was just like everyone else. I grew up with my brothers and sister. I have three brothers and one sister and it was . . . what can I say, just a regular childhood, no problems, no worries." He grew up in a two-bedroom house with his mother, father, three brothers, and one sister. As the oldest son, Eduardo had important family responsibilities. His parents counted on him to be a role model by doing well in school and helping his siblings with their homework. On occasion, he attended parent-teacher conferences for his siblings in his parents' absence when they could not take time off from work. Although he had many adult responsibilities growing up, they allowed him to develop keen leadership skills that he has used throughout his life.

Eduardo attributes his success in life to the constant encouragement he was given as a child growing up. His mother in particular played a big role in motivating him to work hard in school to achieve a better life. As he tells it:

> My parents, especially my mom, I'm extremely grateful for all her motivation and pushing and everything because she's the one who's actually pushed me and made me strive for more. And I'm very grateful because I guess I can say that all my accomplishments are thanks to her. Everything I've done is in some part in thanks to her and my parents saying, "You know what? We want a better life for you. Maybe we couldn't do it, but you can, you just have to try."

His mother not only encouraged him to do well in school, but she also did activities with him as a child that developed his intellectual curiosity. Eduardo remembers making frequent trips to the local library with his mother from the time he was in third grade:

> The local library always had either a puppet show or just reading time. She was always big on making me go and making my brothers go. I would go a lot and, of course, when I had projects. I started going around third grade.

Both of Eduardo's parents were very active in his education growing up. In elementary school, he remembers his parents being very involved in school activities. He says, "My parents were very involved, and my mom was always big on bringing stuff." With all that support and encouragement, it was only natural that Eduardo excelled in school at a very early age.

Eduardo is very proud of all of his academic accomplishments. He explains, "Since elementary school, I received a lot of certificates, Scholar of the Month, Citizen of the Month, academic achievement, mathematic excellence." He is most proud of his big academic accomplishment in middle school, "I had a lot of accomplishments in middle school. Eighth grade was my best year. I was salutatorian, so that was awesome. I'm most proud of my salutatorian award." In addition to excelling in school, he was very involved in various extracurricular activities. He recounts:

> I was involved in the orchestra since sixth grade. I won the orchestra award for top violinist player in my class, so that was awesome, and I also was involved in a club, called the Olympians. It was sort of like leadership, and I was president and got awarded a plaque for that.

Eduardo has always taken on leadership roles in the student organizations in which he participates. He enjoys the opportunity to develop his leadership skills, a theme that defined his high school career. One of the programs Eduardo was very involved in during high school that gave him the opportunity to develop his leadership talents was ROTC:

I was involved in Junior ROTC, and I just developed a lot of leadership skills, and I became a better public speaker because it's difficult some-times speaking in front of a large crowd. But I guess I kind of started getting used to it. One of the biggest events I remember in high school was this event, called the All City Staff Competition, and that's an event where each school selects the top eight cadets, and they send them out to compete against other schools, so they can elect ten staff personnel and I was selected amongst those from my school. We sent out only four, and only two actually went, so I was amongst those two and I came out number five in the district. That was one of the biggest events I remember.

Eduardo also held an important leadership position in ROTC during his participation. He says, "I was a captain, and top ranked were captain and major, so you couldn't go higher than that." His desire to hone his leadership skills also led him to run for office in other organizations. He recalls, "I joined student government where I was elected class president. I also was part of the National Honor Society, where also I was elected president, and was invited into the California Scholarship Federation." He is very proud of the many leadership positions he held in high school.

In addition to his extracurricular activities, Eduardo was a top aca-demic scholar in high school. As such, he received many awards, including:

> I actually got perfect attendance, academic achievement. I was Crimson Scholar and got a Gold Seal Bearer, received a National Honor Society award. I participated in the Science Fair, where my team came in third place. In ROTC, I was Cadet of the Year.

Eduardo also took numerous academically rigorous courses, "Junior year, I took AP statistics, AP U.S. history, AP English, and AP chemistry. Senior year, I took AP calculus, AP physics, AP English, and AP government."

Being such a prominent leader on his high school campus got Eduardo noticed by both teachers and administrators. As a result, he was able to establish a strong connection to his high school counselor, who was influential in his education. She nominated him for awards and was key in his decision to apply to a summer enrichment program. In fact, this counselor encouraged him to apply for a summer leadership program at a local university. He remembers:

> She always pushed me . . . she always was telling me, "Consider applying here or try doing this" . . . we kind of established this sort of friendship, and she nominated me for an award. She actually told me to participate in this program that USC offered, called the Leadership Initiative in Sacramento.

Eduardo was accepted to the summer program and had a phenomenal educational experience. Another teacher who had an important impact on Eduardo was his English teacher. He was very encouraging, always telling him that he was talented and could do anything:

> He always pushed me, and he was the one who advised me, "Oh, you should run for president. You should do it because I know you can do it." He wrote my letters of recommendation, and he told me to read them, too, because he just didn't want to send them out. So I read what he had to say, and he'd always tell me, "Oh, you know, you're Oxford standard and you're this and that." You know, it was really positive.

After all of the amazing experiences he had in high school, Eduardo left thinking the sky was the limit and, with hard work, any goal he set for himself was attainable. His first year of college, however, he started to think differently as the reality of his undocumented status set in.

So far, college has been very tough for Eduardo. His lack of legal status constantly limits his opportunities as a college student. Since his undocumented status prevents him from obtaining a driver's license, his stepdad has to drive him to and from school, a commute of 48 miles each way. His transportation situation also makes him feel vulnerable about other students discovering his secret:

> It's hard because at school . . . at college right now, for example, when they ask, "Oh, where are you living?" or stuff like that, I say, "Oh, I'm a commuter." So everyone assumes I'm driving, and I'm not about to

explain, "Oh, no, my dad drops me off." It's really none of their business, and at the same time, I feel like I'm deceiving them and I'm lying.

His lack of transportation limits his flexibility to participate in extracurricular activities, a very sensitive issue. He explains that he had joined one student club his first year of college, called Chicanos and Latinos for Community Medicine, but had to stop because meetings were held on days he was not on campus:

> Unfortunately, the meetings changed so I can't attend because I'm only there Monday, Wednesday, Friday. And the meetings now are Tuesdays, and I just can't go all the way over there for an hour of the meeting, so it's tough because I'm restricted in joining clubs, participating in school events, taking on leadership roles, and I think it's a bit damaging in the long run.

Another challenge Eduardo faces in college is balancing school with work. He says:

> I have a part-time job and I work on days that I don't go to school, so I'm working on Thursday, Saturday, and Sunday. I try to help out financially because I also need the little extra help to buy my books or buy things I need.

Since he is responsible for paying for his own tuition, he has to make sure he is always working. Eduardo did receive a scholarship from a local nonprofit organization that helped him pay for some of his expenses during his first year of college. Like other undocumented students, Eduardo has been resourceful in finding scholarships that do not require legal citizenship.

In the future, Eduardo hopes to pursue medical school after earning his bachelor's degree. He declares, "I really want to get into medical school and become a physician, family practice, and help unprivileged families if I can. I think that would be a big contribution because we need people to help out." As a doctor, Eduardo will continue to use his leadership talents to help the communities most in need. For now, however, Eduardo clings to the hope that immigration reform will be passed, allowing him to pursue his career as a doctor. He says, "I have high hopes that something along those lines reestablishes where I could apply and be granted some sort of residency, and that's what I'm hoping for, and that's why my career plans are still on track."

12 RAUL

"I am always limited in what I can do."

BEING undocumented has taught Raul a valuable life lesson: "Don't take *anything* for granted." With this in mind, Raul takes advantage of every educational opportunity possible. He says, "Because of my status, I understand what I can't do, and because of that I take the things that I can do more seriously. I can go to school. I can get good grades. I take pride in being able to do that." Although Raul is aware that being undocumented puts obstacles in his path, this realization makes him work even harder to accomplish his educational goals.

Raul was four years old when he came to the United States. As a child, he grew up with his mom and three older brothers. He describes his childhood as "difficult," growing up in a single-parent household as an undocumented immigrant in a low-income community. When he was young, Raul had a significant life experience that solidified his decision to go to college. He recounts:

> We were playing soccer outside because I live in a not-so-good neighborhood, and there was a drive-by [shooting] right next to us. That is when I realized that I need to get myself and my family out of here and education is the way. I am not going to be able to get out of here if I enter the workforce right now, especially because at that point I knew that college was the only way.

From that moment on, Raul did everything he could to prepare for college, not an easy task for someone who started school with limited English proficiency. Nevertheless, his determination got him through and on the road to academic success.

When Raul started elementary school, he was placed in regular mainstream classes even though English was not his first language. He recalls, "I remember having to learn the language as I went along, and at no point did I take an ESL [English as a second language] class." Being placed immediately in all English classes made Raul's adjustment to school tough. He had to master English as quickly as possible. Despite this stressful situation, Raul quickly mastered English and was enrolled in the GATE program, demonstrating his ability to excel.

As early as elementary school, Raul was involved in extracurricular activities, such as student council, which gave him the opportunity to connect with his teachers. Two of those elementary school teachers were very influential early on and continued to support Raul beyond elementary school:

> My second-grade teacher, who I actually still keep in touch with, was always very helpful. During the summers, I would go to his classroom to help. Also, my third-grade teacher, she actually bought me a laptop before I went to college.

Raul earned his teacher's admiration because she saw his diligence and dedication to succeed.

His record of high academic achievement and involvement in extracurricular activities continued in middle school. Raul was involved in activities such as "mediation, which is a peer counseling group, and drama." He also excelled academically and always made the honor roll. He explains, "I made the principal's honor roll every year up until the eighth grade except for one trimester." Similar to elementary school, Raul had one influential teacher who supported and encouraged him to set higher expectations for himself:

> One of my math teachers. He was the one that wanted me to do more. He noticed that I was a good student but settled to be average. He told me that it was going to get me somewhere but not as far as it could.

This stuck with Raul, and from that moment on, he doubled his efforts and pushed himself harder in school.

In high school, Raul's dedication and hard work paid off when he graduated valedictorian of his senior class. He also received numerous academic awards, including "an award from the math department and one from the English department." Raul was very active in extracurricular activities in high school, saying, "I did academic decathlon my senior year. I did mock trial my freshman year. I did mock trial because I want to be a lawyer, so as soon as they posted the fliers, I signed up." Raul's participation on the academic decathlon team significantly influenced his educational goals. He was most proud that his team performed so well in light of the fact that they had fewer resources than most of the schools they competed against:

> We are one of the poorest schools, and during the school year we all studied hard. We all put in a lot of work, and although we didn't win, we moved up fifteen spots and we beat some of the other local schools who thought they were better. We got to show them what honor students like us can do.

Even though his team was the underdog in competitions, the members still worked hard to place as high as they possibly could.

During the summer before his senior year in high school, Raul was chosen to participate in a prestigious summer program, called the California Boys State. He was nominated by his counselor and then selected from among a group of seven juniors to represent his high school. He describes his experience:

> They take male students, the summer of junior year. They take them onto a campus at one of the California schools, and you become the government. So they put you in the dorm room, and that dorm room is a county, and each floor is a city. So you pick city officials and then you get elected to Congress.

Raul was very excited when he learned that he had been selected for the program. He knew this wonderful opportunity would get him one step closer to his goal of going to college.

Raul acknowledges the many teachers who have helped him achieve his goal of getting into college. Much like in elementary and middle school, Raul found a teacher in high school who showed an interest in his academic success. His senior year, he found a teacher who helped him navigate the struggles of applying to college as an undocumented student. He describes his English teacher's influence on his college goals:

> She was the one who told me, "Even though you have this status, you can still go somewhere. We are all going to help." She would go home and do research and come back and be like, "These are the schools you can get into. These are the schools that don't ask about your status. This is where you can get scholarships and grants from." She really helped me a lot.

Raul realized that with dedication, there was a way to achieve his goal. With the help of his teacher, he was accepted to a prestigious four-year college and was ready for the new chapter in his life that he had worked diligently toward for many years.

Now in college, Raul faces new challenges, many of which are still the result of his lack of legal status in this country. Like most undocumented students, Raul says the hardest part of college is seeing the opportunities other students who are citizens are able to pursue that he cannot:

> I see the differences between me and the rest of my classmates. When the summer comes, everyone is talking about what internships they should get, or "I'm going to go study abroad in France or in South Korea." So when they would ask me, I would have to say, "I'm going to go home." So that's one of the things that comes up a lot, a lot of differences in what I am going to do compared to my classmates.

The discrepancy between Raul and his U.S.-citizen classmates seems more pronounced in college. He feels that the higher up on the educational ladder he goes, the more visible the opportunities closed off to him become. Although Raul sees this inequality, and realizes all the limitations that come with being undocumented, he still persists:

> It has been a bit difficult because I am always limited in what I can do. In college, I was offered two jobs, which I couldn't take because I was

undocumented. There were also internships that I couldn't take. Driving to the university was a difficult challenge. Things like that, things that most people don't think about.

Even though Raul faces many challenges in college because he is undocumented, he is still very involved in extracurricular activities on his campus, including "RAZA, a Mexican American club. I am in a club, called the Black Man's Forum. I also hope to build a drama production group. I am also in a fraternity." In addition to his academics and activities, Raul works in college to pay for his tuition. He says, "I work at the student grill. I always work late, from 10:00 pm to 1:00 am. It was hard, but it was the only job that I could get because they pay in cash."

Regardless of the countless barriers in his path, Raul continues to work toward his college degree to achieve his long-term career plans. His educational goal in the future is "to get into a law school. It's my mom's dream to have a lawyer in the family." In fact, Raul often uses his mother, who has struggled to support him as a single parent, to motivate him. He explains, "One time I was complaining, while my mother's still supporting three children and working as a babysitter, so it's, like, I have no right to complain. So that helps to keep me humble and focused." The most disappointing aspect of being undocumented for Raul is "realizing that if I stay undocumented after my four years of college, I will be a college graduate who cannot find work." Raul hopes this will not be his story after working so hard to earn his college degree.

PART FOUR

College Graduates

13 <u>LUCIA</u>

*"The biggest disappointment is knowing that there's
no light at the end of the tunnel."*

LISTENING to Lucia's long list of educational accomplishments, it is hard to believe she made her way through the educational system with limited resources as an undocumented student. She is just one of the thousands of high-achieving immigrant students who graduate from American high schools each year, but have limited college prospects due to their lack of legal status. Despite the many obstacles Lucia has faced, her story is one of a never-ending search to find the light of U.S. citizenship at the end of her tunnel.

Lucia's story is motivational and inspiring. She came to the United States with her parents when she was seven years old. As she was about to finish second grade in Mexico, her parents told her they had decided to make the journey to the United States. Although she was perfectly happy living in the small town in Mexico where she was born, her father felt that there were not enough opportunities to provide for his family, and much to Lucia's dismay, the family would be making the journey north in search of a better future. It was decided that her father would leave first, and Lucia, her sister, and mother would follow.

Leaving everything familiar behind—her town, school, family, and friends—Lucia braced herself for her new life in the United States. She was scared, as any child her age would be, for in what seemed like the blink of an eye, she was immersed in a new and unfamiliar place that often left her feeling like a fish out of water. Two of her toughest challenges lay ahead for young Lucia, starting school and mastering English.

From the moment she set foot in her new school, she knew that she was very different from her American classmates. Everything was unlike her school in Mexico. While she described her school in Mexico with feelings of joy, saying, "I think school was fun. I loved it," her description of school in the United States was the exact opposite. In very vivid language, she described her early school days as "horrible," and that she felt very out of place:

> It was horrible. I remember the very first week of third grade, I always like to describe it as the Charlie Brown moment where the teacher's going, "Whaa-whaa-whaa," and you don't understand a word she's saying. I sat in the back of the class, and all my classmates were Anglo. My teacher was very, very mean. She didn't like us and made sure we didn't speak Spanish in the classroom. Anytime she caught us speaking Spanish, she would knock something down, like a ruler on the desk, and she would say, "We do not speak Spanish here. You do that on your off-time!"

Learning in a new language was a challenge for Lucia. Her description of her initial schooling experience is interesting because she refers to a quintessential American cartoon—Charlie Brown—to describe how she felt as a Spanish-speaking immigrant child thrown into the American educational system. Her Charlie Brown reference clearly speaks to her American cultural orientation.

Knowing that she was in for one of the toughest challenges of her life, Lucia began to use the resourcefulness and determination that was so evident throughout her story. She immediately looked for allies, people who could help her learn English as quickly as possible. She describes how a classmate became her personal translator:

> There was one girl who sat by me in the back, and she kind of had a Mexican last name, but I thought, "She doesn't really look Mexican." She looked at me kind of weird, but then, when I started talking to her, she told me she understands some Spanish and she would try to help me, and so she was very friendly and she knew English. English was her first language, but her grandmother spoke Spanish and her grandmother was her babysitter, and so she kind of knew some Spanish. She would

help me try to understand as much as she could translate from the teacher and help me do some of the homework and understand it.

It is truly ironic that Lucia has worked so hard and has been so motivated to master aspects of American culture, such as becoming fluent in English, yet she still finds herself on the margins of American society due to her lack of legal status. It is also quite amazing that, even under negative circumstances, her love for school and learning has persisted in the face of adversity. Even at such a young age, Lucia was hopeful that a reward awaited her, a bright light at the end of her educational tunnel.

It was not until her freshman year in high school, when Lucia was starting to prepare for college, that she had to face the reality of being undocumented. In the back of her mind, she said, she always knew she was not here legally, but when she realized it would affect her dreams of going to college, then it really sank in. When she was filling out the forms to take the SAT and asked her mom for her Social Security number, her biggest fear was confirmed:

> I always knew it, but I didn't want to accept it. Having my parents tell me was really hard because I thought, "Forget it then, I don't need to take the SATs, and I don't need to take those things for college."

Although Lucia's spirits fell after learning about her undocumented status, she did not stop working hard and excelling in school. She forged on. Her academic accomplishments in high school alone illuminate her persistence and hope that she could still reach the light at the end of the tunnel. Lucia graduated in the top 50 of her class of a thousand students with a GPA of 3.89. She also received numerous academic awards because she was such an outstanding student. She recalls:

> I got a lot of awards in high school. I won the Compact Scholarship, the Northside Impact Scholarship, and then I also got the "Friendliest Face in the Family" award, because no matter what anybody said, I always kept a smile on my face. I also got the "Most Passionate in the Family" award because I always had something I was passionate about or a cause I was fighting for. I got Outstanding Student of the Year my senior year. They also gave me the "Multicultural Award" because I

brought in a Chicano muralist from L.A. and, together with MEChA [Movimento Estudiantil Chicano de Aztlán] and the community, we raised thirty-seven thousand dollars so we could put a really large, multicultural mural on our campus.

Lucia was also very involved in extracurricular activities in high school, often taking on leadership roles for which she received numerous distinctions:

> I joined mock trial in high school and we won . . . we were state champions in 1998, and I was the lead prosecuting attorney and I was star witness. I got state awards for being the best defense witness. I joined speech and debate, and I did academic decathlon.

In high school, Lucia was also involved in the Associated Student Body (ASB) and MEChA. It was during this time that she got more involved with volunteering, community service, and many other important civic activities:

> I would go to the convalescent home and volunteer there every summer because I loved it. I loved working with the elderly, and I was in charge of playing games with them, so that was even more fun for me because I got to play bingo with them and teach them new things.

Since high school, Lucia has continued to volunteer and perform community service. In fact, I interviewed her during a two-hour break she had while running a weekend leadership workshop for high school students.

Lucia's journey through the educational system has been anything but easy. When she graduated from high school, she was accepted to UC Berkeley, the best and arguably the most prestigious public university in the world. But when she could not provide them with a Social Security number, they withdrew her acceptance. Although this situation enraged her, it also renewed her motivation to succeed and continue to work toward her long-term career goals:

> I was like, "I don't care if Berkeley doesn't want me. I'm going to do something else"; so I used my connections. I just talked to everybody

and anybody I knew. I would tell them my story, and they would follow up with me, and they would say, "I don't know how we're going to help you, but we're going to help you." And they would do things like give me scholarships and just things like that.

Similar to when Lucia was in elementary school, she skillfully sought out help from others. She is a social butterfly and so articulate that people cannot help but be sympathetic to her plight because she is so hard-working and ambitious. Since high school, Lucia has often relied on the kindness of strangers. She explains some of the generous gifts she received from teachers at her high school:

They would be, like, "Here, we're paying for your prom," or just things that they knew would help me out. I got that from a whole bunch of people everywhere I went. My high school history teacher paid for my grad night ticket; my other high school teacher paid for my class ring.

At the community college, she continued to meet other kind souls who helped her pay for school because she had to pay higher tuition fees than everyone else. Because of her undocumented status she had to pay $142 a unit, while her U.S.-born classmates only paid $10 a unit. She describes the kindness of a woman she worked for who assisted her when she was enrolled in community college:

I met a really nice lady who I just ended up taking care of her kids. She was a blessing because I got to clean her house and take care of her kids, and she would give me money for college. I always knew she paid me more than she should have, and she knew that too, but she knew where the money was going, so she would always tell me, "Don't worry. I'll pay for your first semester" or "I'll pay for your second semester." She helped me get another job where they paid me in cash.

As this story demonstrates, Lucia often had to find jobs that paid her "under the table," such as cleaning houses or taking care of people's children, because her status prevented her from getting a regular job. She always worked multiple jobs to make sure she had money for her tuition so she could stay in college:

I had to learn how to hustle. I had to do whatever I could do, anything to get a job. I would clean houses, take care of people's kids, mow lawns, anything just to make sure I got that money to pay for the classes every quarter.

After a little over two years, Lucia was able to transfer to a local public, four-year university. Even though she was accepted easily to the university based on her academic credentials, her challenge was paying the out-of-state tuition that was required because she was not a U.S. citizen. Just as she had done before at the community college, she hustled to find jobs to pay her tuition each semester. Lucia always worked more than 40 hours a week, juggling multiple jobs during college to earn enough money to attend school full time. She explains:

I would take care of kids. I did a lot of tutoring for little kids, and that helped me pay the bills. I even worked for a dot-com at some point doing college recruiting. It was like a college information website with free e-mail for students or whatever, and somehow I got hired. I don't even know how that happened, but I would be on campus posting up all these posters for students to sign up to this thing, and I would just get paychecks every month, and that was wonderful. I did whatever I could to hustle.

Even though she was working and going to school full time, Lucia always found time to contribute to her community and become involved in social and political issues. Throughout her life, she has always been very involved in politics. She says:

I was always talking to a legislator or a community official. I volunteered in every political campaign in my area. Anytime there was an opportunity to help a Democratic candidate, I would help them. I even helped one Republican candidate because I just thought he was amazing, and I didn't care he was a Republican. I helped in the elections for every congressperson in my area, every assemblyperson, every mayoral election. I even helped with the attorney general campaign, and I did one of the Davis campaigns. I was involved in school board elections like crazy. I did the whole painstaking labor of walking house-to-house and knocking on doors and telling people why they should vote for the candidate we were supporting. For my efforts, I got Outstanding Volunteer of the Campaign awards because I was there all the time, and I didn't care if I had to take two buses to get to that campaign headquarters. I did it.

Lucia has managed to overcome numerous obstacles in her path and accomplish many, but not all, of her educational goals. She has earned a master's degree, but still hopes to attend law school and become a lawyer. For Lucia, the hardest part of being undocumented is that she has worked so hard in school, but her bachelor's and master's degrees cannot give her what she desperately needs and has earned with her countless contributions to American society:

> The biggest disappointment is knowing that there's no light at the end of the tunnel. Knowing that it doesn't matter how many degrees you get, it doesn't matter. At the end of my degree, there was no job for me. There was no job for my family. There was no way of me putting all this education to use that I had paid for by cleaning houses and taking care of people's kids. That has definitely been the most challenging part.

At the end of my conversation with Lucia, it seemed like the light at the end of the tunnel that had seemed so bright when she was in elementary school had dimmed considerably and, sadly, may not rekindle. She feels as though she is being punished for a decision her parents made many years ago to come to the United States in pursuit of the American dream:

> I wasn't asked to be brought here. I didn't choose to come here. I didn't ask for my situation. I feel like it's a punishment. I did everything I was told to do. I stayed out of trouble. I stayed out of gangs. I didn't get pregnant at sixteen. I'm a great member of society. I know more of civic duty than most naturalized or U.S.-born citizens. I know more about politics than most U.S. citizens. So why am I being punished?

14 MICHAEL

"It's like a wound that never heals."

MICHAEL is determined to become a doctor. When I interviewed him, he was in graduate school working on a master's degree in public health. His journey to graduate school has not been easy. During his first years of college, he was paying high international student tuition fees. It was not until his second year that he was relieved of the high tuition cost when California's in-state tuition legislation took effect. Despite the many challenges Michael has faced as an undocumented student, he continues to make his way successfully through the educational system. He describes being undocumented, "It's like a wound that never heals that you learn to deal with." For Michael, the sense of rejection hurts, but he has learned to cope with the reality that his legal status may never fully "heal."

Michael was eight years old when he came to the United States with his parents. He is the oldest of four siblings. Michael's parents were clothing merchants in Mexico and owned two clothing stores. Even though, as entrepreneurs, Michael's parents did well for themselves, they still valued education highly and made sure their children knew they needed to go to college. Growing up, Michael's parents played a key role in his educational goals. He explains:

> I decided I wanted to go to college ever since I was in fifth grade. My mom and my dad would talk to me. They would tell me, "You're going to go to college, you're going to go to the university." They are the most influential people in my life. It goes beyond just playing the mom and the dad. It's way beyond what I would consider a normal parent

would do. For them, no matter what, education was first. If they had to remortgage the house so that we could go to college, that was fine. If they had to find an extra job so they could help me pay for college, that was fine. They would never tell me that you need to work because we need extra income for the house.

Michael parent's were willing to do just about anything to make sure that he got a good education and attended college in the United States. He wanted to succeed, of course, and make his parents proud.

Michael attended elementary school up to second grade in Mexico. When he started school in the United States, he was immediately placed in the ESL program. Although Michael's initial experiences in the American educational system were tough, he still worked hard to excel academically. By the time he reached high school, Michael was taking honors and AP courses and receiving numerous awards. He says, "I got several straight-A awards. I got a couple of medals for outstanding participation in Associated Student Body, and community service awards because I was doing a lot of community service back then." He also participated in various extracurricular activities: "In high school, I was very involved. I played baseball. I was in ASB for two years. I was president of MEChA. I was in MEChA all four years. I was also in the key club." As a result of Michael's active engagement in high school, he was selected to participate in a precollege academic enrichment program at a prestigious university. That summer experience led Michael to aspire to become a doctor. He recalls:

> I was in a precollege program. I was invited to several leadership camps. I would take classes during the summer and would stay at the dorms of the university. My junior year I was already taking some calculus courses with them. They would take us to different places. This program had a math and science emphasis, so you could go to the coroner's office, medical schools, all that. It was awesome. I went there for three summers, until the summer before my senior year.

In addition to his academics and extracurricular activities, Michael worked starting his junior year at a local toy store.

The last two years of high school are always heartbreaking for undocumented students, and they were no different for Michael. His senior year,
Michael had been accepted to many prestigious universities, none of
which he could attend because the tuition cost was beyond his ability to
pay, and he could not get any financial aid. He explains:

> I remember out of high school I had been accepted to seven different
> universities, and I had already picked one in northern California to go
> to, but my situation wouldn't let me go. All the universities sent docu-
> ments saying, "You can't go. You are going to be considered to be an
> out-of-state student." Where the heck are we going to get the money
> from?

Temporarily demoralized, Michael ended up attending a community college, which he felt was a good experience because the school had many
programs to help undocumented students. He says, "I remember sometimes they would find a way to give me a stipend to buy books and all
that. It was kind of like a sanctuary because at that time there wasn't any
in-state tuition law." Michael worked very hard in community college
because he planned to transfer to a four-year university quickly, which
he did.

The first year Michael attended a four-year university was very difficult
financially because it was a year before the in-state tuition law took effect,
and he was paying out-of-state tuition. He also had a tough commute to
school. He says, "I was actually taking a carpool. I remember I would
wake up at 5:00 am in the morning every day so that I could pick up the
van at 6:00 am." At the university, he participated in a fraternity and
studied molecular, cell, and developmental biology in hopes of attaining
his goal of becoming a doctor.

Without financial aid, Michael had to work, "thirty to thirty-five hours
a week" to pay for college. At one point, he found a great job at a research
laboratory that paid well, but he was forced to leave because of his lack
of legal status:

> I worked a lot, but I was not getting paid a lot. Then I got a job at a
> laboratory, and for the first time I felt like someone recognized the

talent and potential that I had. I was doing a lot of microscope work analyzing DNA and human chromosomes. I was their first person without a college degree to be able to work in that place. So I was making a lot of money when I was working there. But then they found out that I didn't have a [S]ocial [Security number], so they let me go. After that I worked a lot of jobs again. I went back to working in toy stores and retail and going back to work at a furniture store.

Like other undocumented students, Michael missed out on research and internship opportunities because he could not provide a Social Security number to his potential employers. He was also excluded from many educational opportunities for which he was qualified based on his academic record because, he recalls, "I couldn't apply to any programs. I couldn't study abroad. I couldn't do any of those things that I knew I had the grades for, that I was capable of handling. I couldn't apply for internships."

Although he had a bachelor of science degree in molecular biology from one of the most selective public universities in the nation, Michael could not pursue his dream of becoming a doctor, at least not on the same path as other students with his academic credentials. Most future physicians take the medical school entrance exams, apply to several programs, weigh their options, and ultimately select a school that is the best fit. This was not the case for Michael, however, so he paved his own path. While he weighed his options, he decided to enroll in a master's program in public health, bringing him a step closer to his dream.

Michael remains active in his community and has become engaged in political activism to enact laws that recognize him and the thousands of other undocumented students across the country who have deferred their dreams. He says, "I helped start an organization that advocates for undocumented student rights." He remains committed to becoming a medical doctor, but he would also like to do more by running for public office. His struggles have shaped his strong desire to be involved in politics. According to Michael:

> What I want is to be able to give back to my community and create programs, maybe create another nonprofit organization. But the most

important thing to me is to create policy change. Helping someone, tutoring someone is important, but I think the biggest change you can make is at the policy level.

For now however, it is still unclear whether Michael will be able to legalize his status and finally let his wound heal.

15 JULIETA

"Being undocumented is really depressing."

JULIETA's family applied for legal status when she was in elementary school. Fifteen years later, after struggling to pay for college, graduate school, and a teaching credential, Julieta is still waiting. The agony and frustration were evident when I interviewed Julieta on a chilly weekday afternoon in the fall. The backlog of applications from Mexico could take up to 20 years, her lawyer told her, so all she can do is continue to wait.

Before coming to the United States, Julieta recalls a happy childhood despite the fact that her mother had a life-threatening illness, and her family always struggled to pay for the medical expenses:

> I remember that most of my childhood was spent with my grandmother, my father, as well as my sister and two brothers because my mother was sick. She was an inpatient at the main hospital in Mexico City. I knew that we didn't have as much money as the other people in town, but I remember being happy, happy all the time. We had our own house, our own bedrooms, everything belonged to us. Although we were poor, my brothers and I enjoyed walking under the rain because we felt free. It was fun. It was a lot of fun, despite poverty.

Julieta came to the United States when she was nine years old. Her father decided to immigrate in search of better medical treatment for her mom. Julieta explains:

> We decided to come to the United States because my mother was sick. In 1990, she lost both of her kidneys. She had several surgeries to remove kidney stones, but the doctors didn't do a very good job and left

some kidney stones in her system, and it caused an infection. That's why she lost both of her kidneys. In order to stay alive, she needed to go through dialysis treatment or get a kidney transplant. He knew that the U.S. hospitals had the health care that my mother needed, and so he made the decision to take her to California. He brought her first with my younger brother and then, six months later, he returned for us.

Before coming to the United States, Julieta excelled in school in Mexico. She recalls, "I was a good student. Every year they had an event to celebrate the student who had done the best in the whole school for the entire year. I was that person in fourth grade." When she started school here, maintaining her excellent academic record proved to be more difficult than it had been in Mexico. Her adjustment to the American school system presented several difficult challenges. She recounts:

> It was hard because my teacher wouldn't accept my homework in print, she wanted handwriting, and I had never been taught handwriting. I hated reading out loud with the rest of my classmates because, obviously, my pronunciation was awful. I couldn't read, write, or speak English at that point in my life, and some of my classmates laughed at me. I was brought to a place where I was made fun of. I felt like a stranger because I didn't understand the language or the instructions. It was hard, and it took me three years to be able to speak in complete sentences.

Julieta felt very isolated in school when she first started, but as the years passed, she felt more and more comfortable. Even though she became more proficient in English, she was still placed in the ELD program. In middle school, she remembers her ELD classes as mundane and not intellectually challenging:

> All I remember is that I was in the ELD track. Most of the time we just did busywork, which was to read this book, but when you really don't understand the language or instructions, then you're just staring at the pages for a long time. I remember carrying a little pocket dictionary that I bought at Sav-On [Pharmacy] because I would always be translating in my mind. That's how I survived; I literally carried the pocket dictionary with me every day.

Besides her science class, Julieta recalls math as one of the few classes she enjoyed:

> My math class was the most fun class. I was always good in mathematics, but due to the fact that I didn't speak English, I wasn't placed in algebra I in eighth grade. My seventh-grade teacher told me that I would've done great in honors algebra I, but she said that I wasn't placed there because of my language.

Julieta's struggles with the English language often held her back from being in more academically challenging courses. Nevertheless, she received an important academic award when she graduated from middle school. She says, "I finished middle school, and I got the Principal's Award for academics."

Focusing on her schoolwork was not always easy for Julieta when she was growing up. Her family struggled financially and often lived in crowded conditions, where it was difficult for her to find space to do her homework:

> In order to survive, my family has always rented or shared the rent with other families. So pretty much my family lived in one bedroom, and that would be my mother, my sisters, and my two brothers. My father and I would sleep in the living room. So homework was done in that crowded room. It was on the floor when two or three TVs were on at the same time. The house was always very noisy, and the only space I would find was on the carpet in our room.

Despite these hardships, Julieta continued to excel in school, due in part to the effort of teachers who recognized her potential. She was fortunate to have met caring and supportive teachers who went above and beyond to help her. Before starting high school, Julieta took a summer school course where she met a teacher who was also a counselor at the high school she would be attending. Impressed by Julieta's diligence, he encouraged her to sign up for honors courses. Julieta recalls:

> At the end of summer school, Mr. T asked me if I ever thought about attending honors classes. I didn't know what they were, so he explained

it to me, and I decided that I would try it. He told me to come see him on registration day, even though he was not my counselor. He helped me sign up for honors English and honors geography. He had already talked to the teachers who were going to be teaching the honors classes, and he explained to them my background, and they agreed to give me a try.

Julieta passed her probationary period with flying colors. Her counselor had been right about her academic talents. As a result, she remained in honors courses all four years of high school. She also, "ventured off into AP classes; AP U.S. history and also AP Spanish literature." She graduated from high school with a stellar 3.9 GPA, explaining, "I was among the top one hundred students in the district who graduated, so they had a special ceremony for that."

Julieta also participated in various activities in high school. She says, "I joined the academic decathlon team in my sophomore year. I did California Scholarship Federation, so that involves community service as well. So I completed my community service by tutoring. We would also clean up the zoo or other places." Since math was Julieta's passion, she also tutored kids in math:

> I tutored in math after school three times a week for two hours, and I did that my sophomore, junior, and senior year. During my senior year, I also did an after-school tutoring for elementary students at a elementary school near the high school that I attended.

During high school, Julieta established a strong connection to her academic decathlon coach, whose mentoring she very much valued. She explains:

> She was the teacher who helped me out the most. Not only did I have her as a teacher during the day, but she was also my academic decathlon coach. She was friendly and she had the patience to deal with me and she was approachable, and I think we developed a relationship where she was really looking out for me.

It was in high school when Julieta first realized her lack of legal status might affect her ability to go to college. Even though her parents set high expectations for college when she was growing up, she started to have doubts:

> I don't think there was ever any doubt that I was going to college because my father always insisted that I go. When I doubted I would go to college was my senior year. That's when I realized that I was undocumented. It was my senior year when Prop 187 was coming around. That's when I really started to realize that college may not be an option.

Even though Julieta realized her legal status limitations, she still applied and was accepted to several top universities. Because of the cost, however, Julieta could not attend and, instead, enrolled at the local community college where she spent three years. She explains that she enjoyed her community college experience, "The community college that I attended was like home. There were other students like me, and I had some of the best teachers that I've ever had." She was accepted into the honors program but could not take the night courses because they conflicted with her bus schedule. She did participate in student government, however, which allowed her to make important connections that helped her transfer. She says:

> My second year, I got involved in student government. Being in student government made it fun for me, and it was very important for me because that's when I started to network. It was the advisers, teachers, and administrators that I networked with who were key in getting me transferred to a four-year university. Because the assembly bill AB540 didn't exist yet meant that pretty much, if I didn't have the money, I couldn't finish my bachelor's degree.

Julieta worked on the weekends to pay for her tuition, explaining, "I started working during my college years on the weekends. I would work eight hours on Saturday and another eight hours on Sunday. My job pretty much was to take care of an elderly woman at her son's house." She also received several scholarships that helped her with her college costs, "I got an award for men and women in science. Two hundred fifty dollars is nothing compared to all the money that I had to pay, but it motivated me to finish my degree in mathematics." In community college, Julieta once again met a supportive counselor who encouraged her to continue with her education despite her legal status. She recalls:

> I met one counselor who took an interest in me. He knew about my legal status. He knew there was nothing he could really do to help me out, but he didn't discourage me from pursuing my education. He told me to apply to any school that I could. He's also the one who encouraged me to join student council so I can have something on my transcripts other than just academics. He told me, despite my status, I would get far in life, whereas my other counselors would never tell me that.

When Julieta transferred to a four-year university, it was initially under the extended education program to save some money on tuition. Despite the initial adjustment, she managed to maintain a high GPA, saying, "Academically it was a challenge. But I survived well and I always had at least [a] 3.4 or above GPA." On Sundays she taught mathematics to adults, "I was teaching mathematics to adults in a special program in the community." Julieta lived at home with her parents throughout college and commuted to campus to save money.

After Julieta graduated from college with a bachelor's degree in mathematics, she and her family were still waiting for their legalization application to be processed. Since she still did not have a work permit, she decided to enroll in a teaching credential program because she knew she wanted to become a teacher. Through some connections, she was accepted to a "special program at a private university, and they paid for seventy-five percent of my tuition." Her father kindly assisted her with paying the other 25 percent. Julieta still did not have a work permit after finishing her teaching program, so she stayed at the same university to get her master's degree. She explains, "I decided to get my master's degree in mathematics because I knew I eventually want to teach at the community college." When I interviewed her, she was a year and half into her graduate program, and after 15 years of waiting, still did not have any prospect of legalizing her status.

Beginning in high school, Julieta began to see the importance of having supportive teachers. She has been able to overcome most of the

obstacles in her educational journey by drawing on those supportive rela-
tionships. She recounts:

> The only reason why I have been able to make it through school was
> networking. It's not how much you know, it's who you know. Who do
> you know, who's going to help you out, who is willing to refer you to
> someone else and that you might have a chance at it.

Despite her best efforts, Julieta is still locked out of numerous opportunities that could have enriched her educational experiences or lessened her
financial hardships. She sums up:

> Being undocumented is really depressing. It's disappointing that you
> can't take advantage of the programs that are offered. It's frustrating,
> knowing that you are qualified to do research, or join programs that
> require you to be a U.S. citizen. It's really frustrating to run into scholar-
> ships that have the same criteria.

Julieta continues to cling to the hope that someday she will be able to
use her earned degree to teach at the high school or community college
level. She says, "Ten years from now I will be teaching. I might be teaching at community college or I might still be teaching at a high school."
She feels sad that after all her hard work, she still cannot move forward
with her career, and continues to wait. Despite her situation, Julieta's
faith in getting an education does not waiver: "I['d] rather be undocumented and educated than documented and uneducated."

16 ALBA

"I know I want to be a high school math teacher, but I can't."

ALBA has had a long educational journey filled with hopes, dreams, sacrifices, heartaches, and disappointments. For 16 years, she worked her way through the educational system with plans to earn a Ph.D. and become a community college professor. Now, with a bachelor's degree and teaching credential in hand, her undocumented status has completely altered her career plans. Finally losing grips with her dream, Alba is now training to be a dental assistant, in hopes that this specialized vocation will allow her to enter the workforce more easily. Alba's educational journey has been filled with many inspiring moments of courage.

Alba was 10 years old when she came to the United States. She had a difficult childhood living with a father who struggled with alcoholism and a mother who worked constantly to support the family. She recalls:

> We were poor because my dad drank a lot. He had a good job, but all of his money would end up being spent on beers and liquor, and my mom would work full time, so we ended up not seeing her a lot during the nights. After work, she would get home and we would be asleep and she would leave early so we wouldn't see her that often.

Alba's parents separated when her mother came to the United States, and two years later, Alba and her siblings joined her.

According to Alba, "I was the smart one in the family." As early as elementary school, Alba distinguished herself as a top student. She says, "In first grade, when my first report card came—and, they had a zero to ten grading scale in Mexico—and I got a ten on all of them, except one was a nine." When she started school in the United States, maintaining her academic record was tough, however. Alba's transition to middle school was hard and confusing due to her language skills:

> In my first week, I didn't know where the rooms were and all my teachers spoke only English and I didn't know what anyone was saying, so I was lost and then, finally, in the third day, my English teacher asked me in Spanish, "Do you speak English?" And I said, "No," and then she said, "Why are you in this class?" and she sent me to the counselor so I could change my classes. And I had a hard time finding the counselor because I didn't know where anything was, so my counselor finally changed my classes to ESL.

After being placed on the ESL course schedule, Alba felt very disconnected from the social scene at school. As a result, she did not participate in academic activities such as leadership. She recounts, "I was going to get into leadership, but that required one of the periods be an elective, but because I was in ESL, we did not have electives."

Although Alba is humble about her academic performance in middle school, she was a top student in her graduating class, earning a spot in a high school magnet program for accelerated students. Alba was very excited about her accomplishment but worried about the many sacrifices she would need to make to attend. The magnet school was far from her home and required long bus rides five days a week. After much consideration, Alba decided to take advantage of attending the prestigious magnet school because she knew that to reach her dream of going to college, she needed to make the sacrifice. Alba reflects on the time it took out of her day to get to and from school, "I traveled two hours to go to school and two hours to come back from school."

Despite her hectic traveling schedule, Alba still excelled academically in high school. She was ranked fifth in her high school graduating class and received numerous scholastic recognitions. She explains:

> If you have a 3.8 or above, they will select students to give jackets of excellence, and so I got one of those. I also got an AP scholar certificate for taking numerous APs and I graduated with honors and got a gold

seal for taking five golden state exams. They would put a stamp of recognition on your diploma. I also got two scholarships to start going to community college.

Alba had a unique experience in the honors and AP program at her school because she was the only Latina taking these academically rigorous courses. As the only Latina surrounded by White and Asian students from middle-class backgrounds, she felt very alone. Her feelings of isolation grew stronger when she was confronted with situations that highlighted her ethnicity and working-class background, as the following illustrates:

> Most honors and AP classes, the majority where White and Asian. In my regular classes, that's where I would see the Latino students. It would be weird because in my history class, the teacher would ask, "What did you talk about at the dinner table?" and I'll be, like, "We really don't have a dinner table, we don't talk about the news, we get home at different times, we can't really sit down at the dinner table and talk." I would feel left out because we didn't really do what the rest of my classmates did.

Regardless of her daily struggles, Alba continued to work hard in school, making the numerous sacrifices needed to reach her educational goals.

One of her most challenging setbacks was during her senior year in high school when she began planning for college. Knowing before that she was undocumented, all of a sudden she realized how severely her status limited her educational mobility. She was struck with the reality that without a Social Security card, there might not be college in her future. If it had not been for the empathy and encouragement of caring teachers and counselors who intervened in her planning, her dream of going to college would have ceased:

> I thought that because I didn't have a Social Security number, I wasn't going to go to college, but then one woman said that I was five in the school ranking and asked, "Where are you going to college?" And I said, "I am not going to college," and she said, "How come you're not going?" So I told her about my status, and she said, "Well, you could

go to community college," and then that's how I started going to community college. But I didn't have money to pay for community college, so she helped me to apply for scholarships and counselors wrote letters for me, and that's how I got money to go to community college.

With her dream still alive, Alba moved forward with applying to community college. After getting some scholarship money and a part-time job to pay the rest of her tuition, Alba was ready to tackle the new challenges of higher education, even if it meant more hardships and heartache. In community college, she once again found herself making travel sacrifices to accomplish her goal. She explains:

> I traveled two hours to go to the community college. I would be in class for one hour and be back on the bus for two hours, to go back home, to go work three hours at a restaurant. Most of my time was spent on the bus going back and forth to my job, then to school, then home again.

Similar to her situation in high school, Alba's travel schedule hindered her ability to be actively engaged on campus. She recalls, "I didn't have time to talk to professors. I had to manage my time. I couldn't waste a second. If I was one second late for the bus, I was late for everything, so I had to be on time to catch buses, to go to class, to get out on time." As a result, Alba did not make many connections with professors or other students at her college, which she regrets as a missed opportunity for self-development. After several years at the community college, Alba was ready to transfer to a four-year university where she could earn a bachelor's degree. She applied and was accepted to a "top university" in the nation. Alba was ready to move forward with her education and to finally accomplish her long-awaited goal of obtaining a college degree.

Alba's university experience came with a new set of positive and negative experiences. One of the biggest challenges she faced was paying the much higher cost of tuition when money was scarce:

> It's hard because sometimes you run out of money and you don't know how you're going to pay for the next quarter. You're always looking for money and thinking ahead about how am I going to do this for the next quarter.

Alba's financial situation always forced her to think one quarter ahead. The positive experience she had at the university was finally finding some time to participate in extracurricular activities on campus, as she explains:

> I was in Folklorico. I was in a group focused on helping undocumented students. I was a part of a political local action group my last year. I was also part of a teacher education program where I volunteered to teach students.

For the first time in her education, Alba was able to become socially and politically involved, which made her very happy. Nonetheless, as she inched closer and closer to graduation, she started to worry about what would happen after college as her legal status had not changed. Alba still had no clear sense of what kind of future awaited her:

> I'm about to be done and wondering what's next. Am I going to be able to work in what I wanted to study for? Will I keep going to school? Where am I going to get the money? You don't know what's going to happen next. You know what you want to do, but it doesn't mean you're going to able to do it because you're undocumented.

Even though Alba made many sacrifices to get her college education, the rewards that should have awaited her did not because her undocumented status was still playing a significant role in her future possibilities. Usually, college graduation marks the beginning of endless options and opportunities for the graduate, but for Alba, it was the beginning of her next heartache and disappointment.

When I interviewed Alba, she was a college graduate. She has earned a college degree, but her government will not give her the legitimacy she needs to use it in the workforce. Alba explains the emotional rollercoaster she has been on since graduating, and how being undocumented has forced her to alter her career plans: "I finished college and I know I want to be a high school math teacher, but I can't teach. Initially, I was doing nothing, I was frustrated, I was depressed, I was sad, and I didn't know what to do next. Now, I started going to school again, but I am going to be a dental assistant." Even though there is a shortage of math teachers across the country, and Alba has a teaching credential in math, she cannot be a teacher. She says, "I have a bachelor's in math and a teaching credential. I was about to get a master's, but I needed to teach full time and I can't because of my status."

With strength and persistence, Alba has no plans to give up on her dreams. Even though her status is uncertain and she doesn't know what the future holds, she clings to the hope that eventually she will earn a Ph.D. and teach at the community college level. At the end of our conversation, I asked Alba what she would say to lawmakers if she had a chance to speak to them directly. She would tell them:

> To have a way for students to legalize their status so we could contribute to this society more because most of us are studying to be teachers or doctors or lawyers. And even if we're finished with our education, it is a waste of talent because we can't really do or participate in the society or in the community as much as we would like.

PART FIVE

Formerly Undocumented College Graduates

17 JESSICA

"I wanted to be a public interest lawyer, the kind that helps the community."

JESSICA's story is markedly different from the 16 preceding stories. Whereas earlier stories reflect the voices of undocumented students still living in the shadows, Jessica's is one of coming into the light of legalization. Although she can reflect on being undocumented in her early education, she can also speak to the numerous educational opportunities she now has access to as a permanent legal resident. Now a lawyer working for a nonprofit organization that advocates for the rights of immigrants, Jessica knows that her story is only possible for others if they, too, get a path to U.S. citizenship. No longer on the margins of American society, Jessica can now fulfill her personal aspirations of making a significant and meaningful contribution to American society.

Jessica was 13 when she came to the United States. She comes from a stable home that gave her a "pretty average, pretty common" childhood growing up. She describes her childhood as, "Pretty happy. I had a very close family. There were a lot of relatives around. I grew up with a lot of my cousins. We lived in the same household for many years."

As Jessica explains, her parents have also been very influential in her educational goals:

> Since I was very little, education has always been very important to us because school has always been very important to my parents. I can remember being in the sixth grade and sitting down and doing my homework after school because my mom was there watching me. The three of us would sit at the table and do our homework, and my mother would be watching us as she was cooking. It was just what we were supposed to do.

Jessica credits her mom as being active in her schooling when she was young, explaining, "My mother was very involved in our schooling, always making sure that every day when we came home, we changed from our uniforms, we had something to eat, and then we did homework." Growing up, Jessica's parents made it clear to her that she had to go to college: "My parents told us that since we were very little we had to get a good education. They always told us that we had to do better than them."

Jessica attended school in Mexico up to the eighth grade and always did well. She recalls, "I was always very good in school so academically it wasn't hard. Over there [Mexico], they give awards for the top three students of the class every year and I would always get one." In seventh grade she was honored for her high grades by being chosen for the color guard, saying, "The kids that are part of the color guard, about six to eight kids, are chosen because of their grades, and it's a big honor to be in that because the whole school knows you're in it."

In the United States, Jessica started second semester of eighth grade. She did not feel school in America was very hard: "It wasn't as rigorous as what I was used to. Whereas before I was taking biology, physics, foreign languages, and music, now I was just learning how to add and subtract." Her biggest adjustment to the American school system was learning English and being treated as if she were not capable of doing the work because she was not fluent. She says, "It was tough because we were placed in the lowest of everything, starting from zero basically. We were placed in ESL classes for half the day. We couldn't speak English, so the assumption was we can't do anything." Jessica felt that teachers underestimated her true capabilities because they used her language proficiency as a measure of her potential.

In high school, Jessica continued to be tracked based on her English-language proficiency and was placed in ESL classes. She did not get put in regular classes until the 11th grade, which she felt was hindering her. She explains, "I didn't get mainstreamed in that class until the eleventh grade, and this put me at a huge disadvantage because I didn't have the classes I needed to go to the university." Jessica wanted to go to college, but with her classes, she was not meeting college admissions requirements. Throughout high school, Jessica felt she was never placed in appropriate-level courses and was in remedial courses where she was not being challenged intellectually. In fact, she only took one AP course in high school, "AP Spanish."

Even though Jessica was not given the opportunity to take an advanced-level curriculum in high school, she still received a scholarship to attend community college her senior year. She recounts, "My twelfth-grade year I got a $500 scholarship to go to community college." Knowing about her lack of legal status, Jessica's high school counselor informed her about the scholarship and encouraged her to apply, "It was my counselor who sat me down to talk to me about my plans after high school. She is the one who told me about the scholarship that they give to new students and she is the one who helped me apply and helped me get in," says Jessica. She adds that her counselor was "very instrumental" in getting her on the path to college:

> She was great. I will never forget this, she said to me, "What do you want to do?" I told her that I thought I wanted to be a flight attendant. She told me that was a good idea, but asked me why I wanted to do that. I said that it was because I wanted to travel around the world. She told me she thought that was great, but she said she thought I would be wasting my potential if I did that. She told me to think about something more challenging. I told her that I always wanted to be a lawyer. She told me she thought that was great and that her son was in law school and asked me if I wanted to meet him. So I met her son, and we talked about going to law school and he talked to me about school. This was the first time I felt that someone said, "You can do it." Once I told her that I wanted to be a lawyer she said, "Okay, let's get you some money to go to the community college."

Without her counselor's support and guidance, Jessica might not have pursued higher education with such persistence, nor might she have thought becoming a lawyer was possible.

After high school, Jessica attended community college for a total of six years before transferring to a four-year university. She was accepted to prestigious public universities after two years of community college, but she could not attend because of her lack of legal status. Even though

Jessica had to take the long route, she does not regret it because she enjoyed her community college experience. She explains:

> I loved it, it was great. You know how people say that high school is the best time of their life? Community college was my best time of my life. It was a very social time. Academically, I could pick whatever classes I wanted and it was up to me to challenge myself. So I wasn't restricted by a counselor putting me in beginning math like in high school. I could pretty much do whatever I wanted.

Jessica excelled academically in community college and earned a 3.8 GPA. She also received numerous awards. "I got a lot of scholarships based on merit." She says, "Through the honor society, I always got state awards and scholarships. I became the queen of scholarships, anything and everything that I could apply to, I did." She was also very involved in activities on campus, explaining, "I got really involved in the honor society. I was in student council. I held a lot of leadership positions. I did a lot of community service and volunteering. I did work inside of school, outside of school." Jessica also felt that she was able to make connections to other students and her professors in community college: "I had an extended network of friends and I was close to a lot of professors. It was just a completely different experience than high school." For the very first time in her life, Jessica felt a strong sense of belonging to a place other than her home.

Jessica believes that her community college experience had a very strong impact on her long-term career goals:

> My whole time at community college was influential because it was when I became aware of the limitations that my status had, and, obviously, that changed me. It made me realize that it wasn't just me. It was a bunch of people. So that was very powerful and led me to immigration work.

After six years at the community college, Jessica's life drastically changed when she became a permanent legal resident. All of a sudden, an entirely new world opened up to her that was filled with endless opportunities. Since she was now able to work, she found a job assisting other Latina/o students at her community college:

> I worked for the transfer honors program and I was a T.A. [teaching assistant]. They got a scholarship to use for Latino first-generation students, putting them in blocks of classes and I was a T.A./mentor to different groups of freshman students. That was a very good experience.

Jessica's job provided her with the opportunity to give back to her community, something she had wanted to do for a long time, but had been unable to since she was undocumented.

In sharp contrast, Jessica describes her four-year college experience as "weird, scary, and strange, but so great to be on my own." It was the first time she was so far away from home (500 miles). Jessica did well academically in college and graduated with a 3.7 GPA. She also received a few academic awards:

> The two big ones were, the graduating class of political science always gives an award for the best research paper and I was nominated as one of the finalists. I didn't win it, but it was just cool to be nominated. The other one was at the Washington, D.C., program I participated in; I was given the research paper award.

Jessica also studied in Washington, D.C., an opportunity that would not have been available to her if she had still been undocumented. She recalls, "I worked for a legal nonprofit organization. I worked with the Mexican American Legal Defense fund. I spent three or four months working thirty-four hours a week and taking classes at night." According to Jessica, it was an honor to be chosen to participate in the D.C. programs: "The D.C. program was very hard to get into so it was a recognition. Everyone applies because everyone wants to do it, but not everyone gets accepted." Thus, Jessica had proven herself an outstanding student in college, setting herself up nicely for admission to professional school.

After college, Jessica was accepted into one of the most prestigious law schools in the country. She describes her experience in law school as "great, but challenging." She felt that she grew a lot as a person in law school, developing a strong interest in social justice issues:

> It also opened up an entire new side of me. I had become very involved politically. I was very active in the community and at the school. I was involved in student council and I was my class representative. I also created a fellowship for Latino incoming students and was the coordinator for that fellowship.

It is not surprising that Jessica received very prestigious academic awards in law school. She explains, "I got a couple of fellowships and scholarships. I was given an award during graduation, the public interest award." Jessica attended law school to become a public interest lawyer to help immigrants who face many of the injustices she faced when she was undocumented in this country:

> I had said before that I wanted to be a public interest lawyer, the one that helps the community. I want to do immigrants rights, obviously because of my experiences and friends and family members who have gone through similar situations. So that's why I went to law school. This was just the ultimate way for me to give back. And what better way than through law, which is so powerful?

After law school, Jessica recalls receiving a fellowship to develop a project at a nonprofit organization: "Another honor I got in law school was a postgrad fellowship. I'm a fellow with a big civil rights organization. I'm a civil rights attorney mainly focused on a language access project for immigrants." After her fellowship ends, Jessica wants to continue working as a lawyer for the same nonprofit organization advocating for the rights of immigrants, "I want to continue what I'm doing, hopefully stay at this organization past my two years because here I can make a significant contribution. If I could do this for the rest of my life, I would be happy."

Reflecting on the challenges she faced as an undocumented student, Jessica states:

Before, the biggest frustration was school. Not being able to transfer, not being able to do what everyone else does and takes for granted. Knowing that I was ready to go to the university and not being able to do that was probably the hardest thing. Also, for over eleven years I couldn't go back to Mexico. When relatives passed away, I couldn't go. So that was very frustrating.

Jessica's journey to legalization highlights the obstacles and missed opportunities undocumented students endure and underscores the amazing societal contributions they can make if given a pathway to citizenship. Like Jessica, undocumented students constantly live in the shadows of our society, but they want to enter the light so they, too, can shine brightly and contribute.

18 JULIA

"I would really like to teach college students,
be involved in the educational system."

JULIA became a legal permanent resident when she was a sophomore in high school. Before she became legal, her plans to attend college seemed uncertain. She explains:

> I didn't know when I was going to get it and I didn't think I was going to get it before going to college. My dad had applied for residency a little bit before we came. It was taking a long time, but once I got it, then college seemed more possible.

Unlike most undocumented students, who pursue college without having legal status, Julia was fortunate enough to have that in place when she applied and, as a result, had many options available. Taking full advantage of her educational opportunities, Julia is now in graduate school working on a Ph.D. in engineering.

From a poor neighborhood in Mexico, Julia came to the United States when she was 13 years old. Similar to her neighborhood, the school she attended in Mexico did not have rich educational resources, not like what she would soon encounter in the United States, "It wasn't a very nice neighborhood where we lived. The schools I went to, they had just built them so we had very little resources," she explains. Even though Julia's school had few resources, she still distinguished herself as an excellent student:

> I remember always being a very good student and being a top student, even though we had so little resources, and I tried to compete in a lot

of academic competitions between schools and I always came out on top. I was like the top student. I got top sixth grader award. In Mexico, at the end of sixth grade, we take an exam, an entry exam. I went to one of the best middle schools, and I was able to pass the exam and do well.

Julia attributes her academic success in school to her family's constant encouragement and support growing up: "I have a supportive family. My dad was always very proud of me and always encouraged me. My mother, too." She describes her parents' role in her educational goals:

They were very supportive. Both my parents really believe in education, even though they didn't get that much themselves. My mom fought very hard with her own parents to finish middle school. They only wanted her to go to sixth grade, but she fought for middle school. And my dad, he didn't continue school, but he was very good. He's still very smart, very intelligent, so they always encouraged me or supported me.

In addition to her parents' being advocates for education, Julia was inspired by their strong work ethic to motivate herself to work hard in school:

Their work ethic is very admirable. They work very hard and they've always done their work, they've always excelled, they always stand out, so they were great role models in that sense, that you always have that work ethic of doing your best no matter what it is that you're doing, and eventually the right opportunity comes up and you take advantage of it and try to improve.

Working hard and doing your best to improve your situation is a motto Julia now lives by. When her family first immigrated to the United States, her father worked delivering pizzas, but also took adult courses at the local community college. Julia explains, "When he came to the United States, he was involved in very simple jobs, delivering pizza and things like that. He worked really hard. He often had two or three jobs. Then he also tried to take college classes." Julia's father was setting an excellent example for his daughter.

Although Julia had an extremely supportive family at home, her transition to school in the United States was very difficult. Like most immigrant students, Julia's biggest challenge adjusting to the American school system was mastering English. She describes her first encounter in an American classroom as:

> . . . really shocking. Even though in seventh grade in Mexico we learned a little English, you're not prepared. Once I came here in eighth grade, they immediately assigned me to English as Second Language classes, so I took a lot of my courses in Spanish, like history was in Spanish. Even though I wasn't able to communicate that well, I was doing well in my classes, especially math and sciences.

In spite of her limited ability to communicate with her teachers, Julia was getting good grades in her classes and starting to make her move as a "top student," much like in Mexico. In fact, Julia was doing so well academically, she was immediately identified to be a part of an academic enrichment program that focused on getting students to college. She recalls:

> So they had this program to help students focus on going to college and doing well in their courses. So because I was doing well, I was invited to be part of that program. They interviewed several students, but most students, including myself, were very scared because immediately they were going to switch us to English classes and everything was going to change, and, actually, I told them I didn't want to be in it. But, fortunately, the counselors there talked to me and tried to convince [me] that it will help me and that I should go back and say yes. So they switched me to [those] classes, and I did really well and actually became one of the top students.

With the guidance and encouragement of her counselors, Julia overcame her initial apprehension about joining the academic program. In retrospect, Julia is thankful her counselors intervened and convinced her to participate because the program provided an outlet for her to start to shine academically in school while building her resume for college. Even though Julia had only a working knowledge of English before she immigrated, she was placed in honors courses in high school after being in the United States for only a year.

In high school, Julia found herself in a situation similar to the one in Mexico in that the school she attended did not have many resources. "The high school I went to," she recalls, "didn't have a lot of resources, so it wasn't one of the best high schools in that area. I was able to excel in that as well and be a top student, even though my English was very limited." Due to her distinguished academic record, Julia received numerous awards: "I always got Principal's Honor Roll. I got the Golden State Examinations Academic Excellence Award. I got a Chicano award. I got a fellowship from the Ford Foundation to go to college." In addition to her scholastic achievements, Julia was very involved in extracurricular activities. She explains:

> I did CSF, California Scholarship Federation. I was involved in the yearbook my junior and senior year. I was involved in dance company my sophomore, junior, and senior year. When I was a junior, a group of students got together to put this page we called the Cultural Page into the school newspaper. It had articles in Spanish that talked about how to get involved, how to get your parents involved. I was one of the leaders for that.

Like other undocumented students, Julia balanced her academics with employment:

> I was a math tutor for an after-school program for students that had ESL classes, so I would teach them math. I worked in the high school computer lab, just helping students to use the Internet. I was the computer lab assistant during lunch and after school.

When I asked Julia how she managed to do so well in high school, she once again credited her parents' work ethic for her accelerated progress in school:

> This is something that my parents taught me very well, the things that you want, you have to work really hard, and I really wanted to learn and I was ambitious in the sense [that] I always wanted to excel. Not just do okay, so I always wanted to excel and . . . so that pushed me to push myself very hard in school.

Even though Julia had a stellar academic record in high school, she still experienced a bumpy road getting to college. In high school, she had negative experiences with counselors who doubted her ability to get accepted to the University of California schools to which she wanted to apply:

> I knew I wanted to go to college, but I had some bad experiences with counselors. I also had people tell me, "You can't, you're not going to make it. It's really hard to go to college," things like that. And I did get kind of sad about it, but, you know, it's nothing new, I heard it before, so I'm going to still do it. At our school the percent of students that go to college is very small. I wanted to go to a UC school, and that's when I started talking to the counselors and then that's when they started telling me, "No, you should go to community college. It's really hard to go there and the requirements are really high." But I applied. I didn't do that well in the SATs, but my GPA made up for the SATs, so when I graduated from high school, I was ranked number 7 out of 300 students. So I applied to UC schools and got accepted.

One thing Julia does not like to be told is, "You can't." People who tell her she cannot accomplish a goal because they assume she is not capable is not something she takes lightly. The fact that Julia's counselors doubted her made her work even harder to succeed and prove them wrong. Sadly, that experience was not an isolated incident in high school. She also had teachers who questioned her academic talent:

> Senior year I'm taking calculus, and there comes a time when you take the AP exam for calculus. I was going to take the AP calculus exam, but at the beginning I wasn't doing very well, so the teacher is like, "Hmm, do you want to take the AP calculus? Are you sure? Why?" You know, he tried to discourage me a lot. He said, "Well, you're not doing that well. Why are you taking it?" It kind of made me very upset at him, so [I said], "I'm going to prove you wrong, that I can do well." So I worked really, really hard. I remember I worked really hard for that exam until I was dreaming about it and it became very clear to me. Out of all the students in the class that took the AP exam, I got the highest AP score, and so I became his "superstar," and he was really happy with me. And then he apologized and said that I proved him wrong.

Nothing makes Julia happier than proving people wrong when they doubt what she can accomplish in school and life.

Now in college, Julia has experienced a difficult adjustment. She has found the academic rigor of her college courses to be very overwhelming, stating, "My first quarter was the hardest, it was a big shock. The classes were really tough." She has developed a support group of college friends who share the same experiences:

> The good thing is that I had a group of friends even before I started college, so that was very helpful. At least I didn't feel by myself. It was a big, big help to have this community that were just like me, trying to succeed, trying to do well, trying to prove people wrong, despite all these obstacles and to support each other. We were very studious, so that was a very good experience, so that helped and, little by little, I got used to the university.

Julia is very strategic about always having people around her who encourage and support her efforts to succeed in school. In middle and high school, she drew support mainly from her parents. Now she gets a significant amount of support from her new academic community in college.

It was in college that Julia started laying the groundwork for her path to graduate school. First, she decided to major in chemical engineering even though she needed to take many classes to fulfill the major. She recounts, "So I started engineering, and engineering students in college have like loads of courses and [are] always busy." Next, she got involved in various research programs that ignited her passion for research: "I did research in chemical engineering and I did an internship for a summer research program at another university in chemical engineering." Finally, Julia worked in college as a tutor and research assistant: "I was a math tutor for five quarters, and one of my research positions was actually a job that I worked about seven hours to eight hours a week," which exposed her to a career as both an educator and researcher. Unlike undocumented students who miss out on opportunities to participate in summer research programs or research positions on campus because of their lack of legal status, Julia was able to take full advantage of these academic opportunities. It was these programs and employment opportunities that got her excited about pursuing graduate school and gave her the experience to be a competitive applicant.

After five years in college, Julia graduated with a degree in chemical engineering. When she finished, Julia was not thinking seriously about continuing on to graduate school because she wanted to fulfill family obligations that awaited her:

> I wasn't thinking about graduate school to be honest. My family started to wonder, "When are you going to work, because everybody here is working, and when are you going to have a real job?" So I really wanted to start working, but then the more I started doing research, the more I started liking it and continuing doing that. So I started thinking about graduate school. I liked the idea, but I worried that I was going to be by myself or that I would have to go away from home and my family.

Despite her initial apprehensions, and with the encouragement of her adviser, Julia applied to graduate school and was accepted into a Ph.D. program in engineering. Although she had lived at home all five years of her undergraduate studies, the graduate school she decided to attended was 600 miles away. She now had to brace herself for a new chapter in her life with many new adventures. One of the most challenging aspects of graduate school for Julia so far is being one of few Latinas in the engineering program at her school. Julia often feels like she "stands out" as a Latina:

> It's engineering, so there's a lot of guys and so, first, I'm a girl, and then I'm actually the only Hispanic student in the engineering courses, so I stand out. Just like in high school, they don't expect that much from me, and I guess I can tell. But at the end, I know I'll prove them wrong eventually, but here it takes more work.

With the odds stacked against her, Julia knows she will succeed, and like always, will end up "on top." At the time of the interview, Julia was in the third year of her doctoral program with plans to complete her Ph.D. in two more years, after which she has the following plans:

> I would really like to teach college students, be involved in the educational system here in California. I know that if I decide to do that, I'll

find different ways to encourage people. Also, since one of the reasons I went to grad school is because I like doing research, I'd like to go into the biotech industry.

In 10 years, Julia sees herself as an educator and mentor:

I definitely want to be someone that can encourage students because I got that, you know, when I was growing up, and that's one of the main reasons why I'm still going to the university. So that, for sure, will be my life in 10 years.

Julia has proven herself as a trailblazer and plans to encourage, support, and mentor others who want to follow in her footsteps. Her outstanding educational accomplishments would not have been possible if she had not been legalized.

19 IGNACIO

"I would probably be working as a truck driver . . . earning minimum wage."

IGNACIO, who recently received a Ph.D. in education, is soft-spoken, kind-hearted, and a vicious competitor. When this country repeatedly rejected, persecuted, and ignored him, he still persevered. The reason he has done so well is because he is a fighter. Ignacio came to the United States in search of a better life after the devastating 1995 earthquake in Mexico. Now, with a doctorate in hand, he has found the life he came looking for in the United States.

The earthquake in Mexico had a devastating effect on Ignacio's family and left his father unemployed. At his father's suggestion, 14-year-old Ignacio made the long journey to the United States to join his sisters. "After the earthquake," Ignacio recalls, "everything collapsed. So I came to the United States. When I first got into San Diego in the morning, I thought, wow, everything was so green! It was a beautiful place." San Diego was a fertile place, full of promise and opportunities, unlike the rubble and despair in his country of birth. Ignacio was optimistic, but that feeling did not last after the novelty of his new surroundings quickly wore off:

> I didn't have anybody my age, nobody to talk to, I didn't speak the language, and I couldn't go out by myself so I stayed home most of the time. After about four or five weeks my sister told me, "Let's go to school." They were taking ESL adult classes. So they took me and signed me up. I studied there for three months until the teacher told me that I could not stay because I belonged in middle school. I didn't want to go because I was happy being there with my sisters and I knew

a lot of people. Finally, my sister said that I needed to go to school, so I signed up and I started halfway through the school year, middle of eighth grade.

Formal schooling was an adjustment for Ignacio. Before coming to the United States, he had not been enrolled in school for more than two years. The last grade he attended was sixth, before a series of life events led him to drop out. Ignacio's initial reaction to formal education was atypical. Judging from his record, one would not have predicted that he was going to reach the top of the educational ladder earning multiple degrees: a teaching credential, a master's degree, and, eventually, a Ph.D. When he was a kid, he hated school, saying, "I didn't like school at all. I would ditch a lot."

Although he hated school, Ignacio loved soccer. His father was the manager and owner of a local men's league team and had nurtured his son's love for the game from an early age. He would often use soccer as an excuse to skip school. Ignacio explains, "Instead of going to school, I used to go to an empty lot and just kick the ball around by myself until my dad found out, and he said that he would have to take me to school instead." Due to his constant truancy, Ignacio's father decided to send him to another elementary school where his aunt worked as a teacher so she could keep an eye on him: "My dad took me there to straighten me out. She was very strict." No one, including Ignacio, would have predicted that soccer, his excuse for skipping school, would someday pay for his college degree in the United States.

Ignacio was a gifted soccer player from a very early age. It was not too long before he started getting invitations from various local soccer clubs to join their team. "They asked me to go and play with them," he says. "We used to play in the city stadium. Also during that time, I was chosen to be on the city's soccer team to represent the city." Soccer also helped Ignacio develop a strong bond with his father: "My dad used to work in the lumber industry up in the mountains. He used to carry down lumber to the sewing mills. Instead of going to school, sometimes my dad would take me with him." Ignacio admired his father so much that he aspired to walk in his footsteps:

I always wanted to be just like him. I remember when I met with my counselor in middle school, she asked me what I would like to be in the future, and I said that I wanted to be a truck driver.

Ignacio's educational path was different from most students'. During his first year of middle school, he experienced a traumatic incident that led him to drop out of school for two years:

> There was one time that me and my friends were walking to school and I was stopped by a car and they ask me to get inside. They were federal undercover agents. So I got in and was scared. They were accusing me of stealing a bike that belonged to a relative of one of the federal agents. In the end, they didn't find anything and they drove me back to school. My mom had to go all the way over there to find out what had happened. I explained to her what had happened; I was crying. After, I got a fever and got sick and I didn't want to go to school.

Afraid for their child's well-being, Ignacio's parents did not force him to go back to school, and, instead, helped him find a job. He recalls:

> After I got better, I took a job with my dad's friend. I used to sand cars before they were painted. They used to pick me up around 3:00 and drop me off around 7:00, so four hours a day, four days a week.

A year after the devastating event, Ignacio was ready to go back to school and took the middle school placement exams. He did very well and was placed in one of the top middle schools in the city: "So, after a year passed I enrolled again. I took the test again and I got into the hard school, so I was taking good classes, but they made me redo the sixth grade." Maybe it was the lingering trauma, or his desire to be with his father, but soon after starting school again, Ignacio left and joined his father transporting lumber to the sawmills:

> I don't know if I got bored or I don't know what it was. I remember talking to my dad, telling him that I didn't want to go to school. So he always gave me the option, "You either go to school or you get a job." And, like I said, I always liked to go with my dad. That is what I wanted

to do, is to be a truck driver. And he said that I could help him out. This was when I was around twelve years old. So we spent the next two years together.

Working as a lumber trucker was a life-changing experience for Ignacio because it was physically demanding labor six days a week. He explains:

> We used to wake up at 3:00 or 4:00 in the morning and drive for two to three hours, get over there and get loaded with lumber, and drive back. We used to get home around 5:00 or 6:00 in the evening. It was hard work for my dad. Rain or shine he had to go to work. He had to load the truck by hand. Each log weighed half a ton. It was very hard. People got killed.

The roads up and down the mountains were very dangerous. Ignacio explains:

> It would be raining at times; there were ravines, and the truck barely fit on the road. He would make me get out and walk in front of the truck, and he used to say, "If anything happens to me, that's me and not you." We prayed every time and we would go really slow. It was very scary for us.

Seeing his father work in a physically demanding and dangerous job gave Ignacio a new perspective on life's struggles. "In retrospect," he says, "I learned that there are going to be obstacles in your life and you have to learn how to take a risk. If you don't take a risk, you're never going to get out." Years later, in San Diego, that insight stayed with Ignacio and he resolved to get to the highest level of education no matter what: "For me, it wasn't enough to just get a BA. Getting a masters degree wasn't enough either."

After almost two and a half years out of school, Ignacio enrolled in middle school again and was placed in the eighth grade. He worked hard that year to do well and master English:

> I was very surprised that I was getting As and Bs the first semester that I was there. And I thought, if I'm getting these grades without even

knowing English, I felt good about myself. I was always very focused on what I was doing and I never thought about giving up. I always thought about things positively. By the end of the year, I wanted to be able to read and write in English. That was my goal.

For the first time in his life, Ignacio was enjoying and excelling in school. Despite his ambitious and competitive nature, Ignacio is a very modest and shy person. He says, "I have always been very introverted. I have never liked personal attention. I always like to just do my job. I don't like to bring attention to myself, and to this day, it's the same thing."

Because he was undocumented for most of his life, Ignacio faced a series of challenges that tested his resolve. He constantly worried about being deported, even when playing soccer at the park on a Sunday afternoon. He remembers, "The border patrol used to come by a lot and pick up a lot of people. They used to do raids." He worried about getting caught and deported not only when he was in public places, but also when he was near his home: "There was a couple of times where they were outside of the apartment where we used to live. We use to relay messages to each other saying not to go outside because there was a federal agent there." The threat of deportation was a daily reality for Ignacio. In fact, several of his family members had been deported on various occasions, so the threat of that happening was real:

> Another time my brother was walking with my cousin and they were chased by border patrol. My cousin got caught, but my brother was able to hide in a trash bin in an alley. So my brother got away, but my cousin didn't; he was sent back. It was a lot of stress because you never knew what was going to happen. The thing that I worried about the most was my parents' being deported because we depended on them, especially my dad.

Despite his daily hardships, Ignacio managed to stay focused on school and soccer, and his commitment to excel in both grew stronger with each passing day. He explains, "I was getting good grades. I was getting five As and one B all the time. There were times that I got straight As." Soccer and school were two complementary forces in Ignacio's life. He did well in school to make sure he always had the grades to stay on the soccer team: "I was getting good grades. I was motivated to go to school. I always took academics first because I knew that if I didn't have the grades, I wouldn't play." In addition to being a good student, Ignacio excelled in soccer: "As a freshman, I was the MVP of the soccer league." At the end of his senior year, Ignacio held his school's record for most goals scored:

> At the end of my fourth year I scored around eighty or ninety goals. It opened doors to other things. There were scouts for private soccer clubs. I remember a Latino coach approached me and told me that there was a guy who was interested in me. He said he would pay for everything. So I joined the team. We used to travel a lot. I was the captain for the club team, and for the high school team, I was captain my junior year.

Like many undocumented students I interviewed, Ignacio also had other obligations besides school and sports. Throughout high school, he had to work to help support his family. He worked as a janitor every evening after school:

> After school, I used to go to work at a retirement home. I was a janitor. I worked there for four years. I would start at 5 pm, and sometimes I would work until midnight. I used to give most of the money to my mom. I kept only twenty dollars to forty dollars. I felt like it was my obligation.

Balancing school, sports, and work was tough, but Ignacio was creative with his schedule. Since he did not have much time to finish his homework after school, he worked on it during his school lunch, explaining, "My lunch was at the library. Every single day I finished my homework there because there was no other time."

Just like Jessica, Julia, and Nicole, Ignacio's life changed forever when he finally legalized his status in 10th grade. No longer hiding from immigration officials, no more constant worrying, but, most important, his path to college was now clear. Although the most prominent barrier was now gone, Ignacio still faced other obstacles in school, starting with teachers who did not always support his college aspirations. Rather than becoming demoralized, however, he used the negative experience to fuel his ambition:

I remember my senior year, my English teacher told me that the way that I was writing, I wasn't going to make it at the university. I thought to myself, "Wow, that's not encouraging!" When I went to the university, I saw her walking on campus. I didn't say anything, but I wanted to say, "Here I am and I am doing great." That experience gave me fire, it encouraged me more. It wasn't just that I wanted to prove it to her; I also wanted to prove it to myself.

For most of his life, soccer had played an important role in Ignacio's life. Initially, it was an excuse to skip school; later it became a way to meet friends and develop a sense of accomplishment. His senior year, he was accepted with a full athletic scholarship into one of the top college soccer programs in the country. It is no surprise that Ignacio received this offer after hearing about his academic success:

So I graduated from high school. I was in the top 10 percent of my class, my GPA was a 3.9. I got a five hundred-dollar scholarship from MEChA, and that year I was also awarded the Student Athlete of the Year for the county. I still remember having my picture in the paper.

Soccer also introduced Ignacio to one of the most influential people in his life, his high school soccer coach, who became like a second father and a close family friend:

He always encouraged me to get good grades and to go to school. When I didn't have my parents here, he was like a father figure. He told me that the only way to make it was to get an education first. He not only helped me, but also my family, my brother, my parents. Advising, encouragement, everything that I needed, he was always there.

When Ignacio went to college, his coach continued to be a constant source of support as he struggled to fit in with his teammates:

He encouraged me during my first year when I felt left out. It was a different environment in college. Most of the players were White, and I was coming from a high school that was mostly Latinos. I didn't feel like I had any support from my teammates. I felt left out. I felt like I didn't belong there, so I talked to him.

Balancing college classes with playing soccer full time was very challenging for Ignacio. On the days when his commitment waivered, he considered his position as a role model for his family and other immigrant Latino students:

> In college, I felt like I was representing my family. At the same time, I felt like I was representing all Latinos. I felt like if I gave up, what would they really say about me? What would my nephew say? So I had to keep going no matter what.

Thinking about his obligation in this way motivated him to persevere.

It is interesting to note that, after having such disdain for school as a child, Ignacio decided during his senior year in college that he wanted to become a teacher, so he started taking courses toward his teaching credential. After he graduated, he worked full time while taking courses part time to complete his credential. Along the way, he also decided to apply to a master's program:

> I applied to one of the local schools here in Los Angeles to get my master's in multilingual education. I was taking one class at a time and finally I passed the CBEST [California Basic Educational Skills Test], and I started substitute teaching. Then I started applying for full-time jobs. They hired me right away, so I started working as an elementary school teacher.

During his years as an elementary and middle school teacher, Ignacio held several leadership positions: "I was the GATE coordinator in elementary school for two years. Right now, this is my third year as a bilingual coordinator at the middle school."

Shortly after embarking on his career as a public school educator, Ignacio earned his master's degree, but he still craved new academic challenges. He had finally discovered his love for learning and was not ready to stop, so he looked to the next level of education he could pursue and applied to doctoral programs:

> I felt like I was missing something in my life. I was missing going to school. I was missing reading books. I enjoyed that. At the same time,

my school principal was applying to a Ph.D. program. She encouraged me to apply with her. I applied, but I didn't get accepted; she did. So I decided to apply to another school and, somehow, luckily, I got accepted.

At the time of the interview, Ignacio had just received a Ph.D. in education. Now, with a deep belief in the transformative power of education, Ignacio wants to become a community college professor to help encourage students to continue their quest for a college degree instead of dropping out to get a regular job. He explains, "I feel like I can make an impact in the community college. I think it's a difficult place because you have to make decisions about either going to work or continuing with your education." As a distinguished teacher who was the first in his family to graduate from high school, college, and graduate school, "Dr." Ignacio reflects on how his life would be different if he had remained undocumented: "I would probably be working as a truck driver or at a low-paying job earning minimum wage." As his story reveals, becoming legalized drastically changed the course of Ignacio's life.

20 NICOLE

"Working with the students who are the most underserved. . . .
that kind of work is very meaningful to me."

FROM being an anxious elementary school student to becoming a doctor of philosophy with a Ph.D. in education, Nicole is a living example of
the promise of the American dream. Her dream would not have become a
reality if she had remained undocumented. As she reflects on her long
educational journey, and the uncertainty that framed her years as an
undocumented student, she notes:

> I would say that if a student's test scores, drive, motivation, good grades,
> responsibility, and potential is based on their success in high school or
> before, then I would say, foster that learning and success so that we have
> more productive individuals in this society. By limiting the education
> of an individual who is undocumented, you are limiting the potential
> of young people who could be great leaders.

As the oldest of five children, Nicole came to the United States as a
four-year-old and attended a public elementary school in Chicago. She
describes her first day in kindergarten as "traumatic." She didn't understand English and felt she had no one to turn to for help. If not for the
aid of a kind and helpful classmate, Nicole would have struggled even
more. She explains, "It was kind of traumatic, but the teachers sat me
next to this other little girl who was of Mexican descent and she would
guide me most of the time. I remember she would translate for me." To
make matters worse, her school was located in a Chicago neighborhood
plagued by poverty and violence. Nicole often feared for her safety on

her way to and from school and even while there: "My elementary school was a really rough school. There was a lot of violence." She was often picked on in the schoolyard by other students, explaining, "It wasn't like hundreds of kids picking on me, it was just two or three kids, but I did sometimes feel taken advantage of." To add to her anxiety, Nicole recalls many experiences with uncaring and verbally abusive teachers. "We had mean teachers," she recalls. "I remember two of my four teachers would constantly scream at us. I just remember feeling so anxious when they would scream like that."

After several years in an urban elementary school, her family moved to a more serene small town in Northern California where Nicole had a vastly different experience. Her anxiety lowered, she finally felt supported, and she could begin to dream. "I remember coming to California, being like, 'Wow, this is so different! Teachers are nice here.' They also had a lot of extra support."

Like most of the students I interviewed, Nicole had to circumvent her school's efforts to keep her out of the college-prep track because they felt she would fail academically rigorous classes. In middle school, Nicole was not on the "newly instituted honors track" despite her high scores on the placement tests. She recalls when a counselor from the high school came to her school to help students pick their ninth-grade courses:

> We took diagnostic tests and I scored really high in math, but my teachers were saying, "Well, you weren't in the advanced class. I don't know if you should try to enroll in advanced class right now. You could try, but I don't know if it's such a good idea." But I still did.

Nicole did not let that counselor steer her away from her dream. Instead, she decided to embrace the challenge.

Having embarked on her quest, Nicole did not have the luxury of dedicating all her available time solely to academics and school activities. Being female and the oldest of five, Nicole always balanced her schoolwork with numerous family responsibilities. She explains:

> I remember coming home from school, and my mom was usually preparing dinner, and I was responsible for watching my younger brothers.

After dinner, I was responsible for the dishes every night. On the weekends, I was responsible for the vacuuming, sweeping, cleaning the bathroom, and helping my mom to do all of the chores.

In elementary school, Nicole's first major obstacle was language, followed by neighborhood violence and poor teachers, all of which caused her much anxiety. Having overcome those obstacles in middle school, her next barrier was the school's tracking system. She experienced her most challenging hurdle in high school when she discovered her undocumented status in 11th grade as she began to prepare for her life as a college student:

> I remember talking to my parents about it and my mom expressing some concern about it. I was telling her I wanted to go to a four-year college and I kept talking about it because I was excited about the idea or the opportunity of just applying. Then I remember her telling me that it wasn't possible for me to go to college because I didn't have papers. I think it was confusing for me because it was a topic that we never really discussed.

Nicole would have to dig deep to find a solution, to find a way to attain her dream. She turned to her teachers for help, hoping they might have the answer, but they did not have much to offer to relieve her worries or console her:

> I remember as a twelfth grader going to my teachers and saying, "I don't know what I'm going to do because I want to go to college, but the thing is that my parents say that we are not legal here so I can't go." My teachers felt bad for me. I remember feeling really bummed about it because I was a good student.

Nicole was an excellent student both in and out of the classroom. Outside of her classes, she pursued various intellectual interests. She was fascinated by languages, so she joined a club with like-minded students: "I was in the foreign language club because I liked learning French and Spanish." She also joined the art club because, she explains, "I like drawing." With her anxiety-ridden days behind her, Nicole also took on leadership roles in those clubs. "I was president of the art club for one year," she relates. Her involvement and student leadership began to be recognized when she received a scholarship from a Sacramento newspaper agency.

Despite her hard work in school and her perseverance in overcoming the growing list of challenges she faced, Nicole had to settle for the consolation prize. She would not be able to attend the university right away because she could not afford it without financial aid. For Nicole, going to the community college felt like defeat and she blamed herself:

> I had to deal with the reality that I was undocumented. I felt naive for not being aware of that. Also, I felt that it could limit my aspirations. It felt like I had worked so hard to be a good student. This was unfair, and I couldn't do anything about it. It was like a feeling of helplessness. I kept telling myself, "I know I'm smart enough to go to a four-year. I know that. But I can't." Accepting defeat, feeling like it's not fair. It's not fair. I didn't feel like too many people were sympathetic, or that many people understood. Maybe even if they expressed concern or felt bad. I just felt like, well, nobody can do anything about it. So what does it matter if people feel bad? It was kind of depressing.

Fighting back feelings of sadness and despair, Nicole had to work very hard not to give up on her dream of going to college. She believed in herself, she had proven her worth, but she was undocumented, so her valiant efforts remained invisible. Despite the setbacks, Nicole remained true to her ambition, working very hard during her two years at community college. She worked long hours to save enough money to pay for her tuition and books, but, with only a few hours left in the day, she was never able to participate in extracurricular activities on campus. In retrospect, she wondered about the lost opportunities for self-growth:

> I just wonder if I could have spent more time in extracurricular activities or maybe traveling abroad or doing something different, more focused on making my academic experience more enriching versus just worrying about whether I was going to be able to keep going to school or not.

After two years at community college, the tenacity Nicole first demonstrated as an elementary school student remained as strong as ever, and she was accepted to UC Berkeley and UC Davis. For the first time, and for the rest of her life, Nicole's educational journey would be different. After 16 years of uncertainty, anxiety, and fear, she and her family received legal status under the amnesty law. The biggest, but not the only, obstacle in her path had now been cleared. As an incoming university student, Nicole was eligible for the financial aid she had worked so hard for 14 years to earn. She thrived as a new college student. She became involved again, this time by participating in a program that helped ethnic minority and low-income students graduate from college and realize their dreams. She says, "I was the peer counselor for a summer program for incoming freshmen. It was meant to increase retention rates of ethnic minority and low-income kids."

It is no surprise that Nicole developed a passion for education as a career. Having accomplished her dream of a college education, she wanted to help others like her do the same. After graduating from college, she went on to graduate school and now holds a doctorate in education. As a newly minted Ph.D., Nicole comments on her ongoing commitment to helping the most marginalized and underserved students accomplish their own version of the American dream:

> For me, meaningful work in the field of education means working with districts or with programs that are targeting low-performing schools and low-performing students. Working with the students who are the most underserved, and the teachers, principals, and districts that serve the students that are most underserved. That kind of work is very meaningful to me. I want to have a presence in conversations when the leaders in my field are having discussions about the plight of English learners and having the opportunity to have a voice in that room.

Nicole's numerous educational accomplishments would not have been possible if she had remained undocumented. Her legal status has allowed her to increase her service exponentially to low-income, immigrant students and an educational system that is in dire need of individuals with her high level of commitment and compassion.

CONCLUSION

Despite the numerous barriers in their paths, Penelope diligently works toward her goal of going to college, Jaime continues to search for a stable place to call home, Jeronimo constantly embraces his American identity, and Lilia remains hopeful that her educational success will provide a pathway to citizenship. These young people are still in high school—their senior year—a pivotal and often memorable year in the lives of students all across the country. For most students, it is a time to dream, hope, and anticipate the rest of their lives. Sadly, it is just the opposite for Penelope, Jamie, Jeronimo, and Lilia. Like the 65,000 undocumented students who graduate from the nation's high schools each year, their future is uncertain, forcing them to draw constantly on their inner strength to maintain a positive outlook.

Most undocumented students cannot muster enough strength to continue their educational ambitions. The barriers are too high, and the struggles too severe. Many abandon their American dream and give up hope. Only one in five of those who graduate from high school continues to battle the daily challenges, the financial worries, and the ongoing struggle in pursuit of higher education. Although qualified for university admission, Daniella enrolled at the more affordable community college. Even though Isabel has been enrolled in community college for longer than she would have wanted, due to financial struggles, she channels her frustration into proactive activities that give her a sense of purpose and belonging. She fully embraces our American ideal of civic participation through political activism focused on immigrant rights. Lucila is a selfless giver. She postponed her college enrollment to volunteer for the Red Cross during the Hurricane Katrina relief efforts in New Orleans, and for the first time felt like an American. Despite her devout commitment to

American society, upon returning to her community college, her feelings of rejection and marginalization resumed. Paulina sleeps in her clothes to begin a daily grind of work, school, and long commute to a community college that does not challenge her enough intellectually. Fortunately, her parents, cousins, and other extended family members have rallied around her to help her pay for school. In many ways, the struggles of the community college students I interviewed mirror the experiences of many U.S.-born, working-class youth who are the first in their family to pursue education beyond high school. They share the same vision of a better future, and one that will be more financially secure than their parents' and grandparents'. They differ, however, in the level of marginalization and exclusion they face daily.

My interviews with undocumented university students opened my eyes to young adults with high levels of psychological resilience and perseverance. Educationally, these students were on the cusp of one of the greatest individual accomplishments in American society—a college degree. Angelica has arrived at this important junction after having to overcome unsupportive teachers and a deep sense of despair that lead her to an emotional low point through most of high school. The passage of the in-state tuition law gave her hope again. Sasha's elementary school teacher called her a "dirty Mexican" and suggested she was mentally retarded, but that did not stop her. As a sophomore in college, with a whirlwind schedule of classes, work, and countless volunteer activities, she has developed a love for government and politics. She yearns to understand why a government that espouses equality and social justice treats her as an inferior outsider. Eduardo, the junior ROTC standout, wants to be a doctor and serve underprivileged families. Raul, the valedictorian, struggles to contain his sense of injustice. Despite his impeccable academic record, all he can do is watch how other students reap the rewards of their hard work, rewards unavailable to him because he is undocumented.

Tragically, the level of despair was highest among the college graduates I interviewed. Even with a college degree in hand, they face grim prospects. Lucia's quest for the elusive light at the end of the tunnel continues with no end in sight. Michael describes his undocumented status as a wound that never heals. Even with a college degree from a prestigious university, and continuing on to graduate studies, his wound remains.

Julieta and Alba, both brilliant math students who dream of becoming math teachers, are unable to get jobs despite having college degrees and teaching credentials. Alba appears to have abandoned her initial dream and has enrolled in a dental assistant program. The stories chronicled in this book beg the question: How long are we going to continue to dehumanize responsible and decent young adults? When are we going to return to our basic principles of equality and social justice?

The testimonies of the fortunate few undocumented individuals who were able to legalize their status provides a glimpse of the life-changing impact of legalization. Jessica, who began her long journey to one of the most prestigious law schools in the country at a community college, is now a rising civil rights attorney. She realized her dream. Despite discouragement from her high school teachers and counselors, Julia attended a top university and is now on her way to a Ph.D. in engineering. She will attain her dream. Ignacio, the middle school dropout who spent over two years out of school before coming to the United States, now holds a Ph.D. in education. He saw his dream come true. Finally, Nicole, who unlike most community college students, went on to earn a Ph.D. in education, was also able to accomplish her dream. For Jessica, Julia, Ignacio, and Nicole, legal status made ALL the difference in attaining their educational goals. It provided them with the constitutionally guaranteed level of equality that is denied to undocumented students. Legal status affirmed their humanity and their place in American society. Thus, we must restore the dignity and humanity of all undocumented youth and their families who continue to endure de facto second-class status in this country.

The stories in this book demonstrate that our immigration laws are broken. They are inconsistent and contradictory. The history of our country has included many laws that today seem unjust and discriminatory. The original laws of this country upheld slavery and limited citizenship to White men. Later laws justified lynching and segregation. Our immigration policies must be grounded in scientific evidence and in a broadly defensible morality instead of irrational fear. Undocumented immigrants take care of our children, our elderly, and our sick. They grow and harvest crops and staff the meatpacking and poultry-processing industries. They build our roads, our schools, and our hospitals. It is time

to reform immigration laws and give dignity to the millions of hardwork-
ing Americans-in-waiting and their children, recognizing that they are,
in many respects, already good citizens of the United States.

Twenty-seven years ago, the Supreme Court affirmed undocumented
students' right to a public education in *Plyer v. Doe* (1982). Since then,
there have been repeated efforts to curtail educational guarantees for students in grades K–12 and beyond. Advocacy has played a crucial role in
the development of legislation that supports immigrant students' right to
attend institutions of higher education at in-state tuition rates. Immigrant students and their supporters have mounted campaigns to educate
the public, pressure school administrators, lobby legislators, and challenge discriminatory laws. Their efforts, which are ongoing, have helped
bring about the passage of unprecedented state- and national-level legislative initiatives, creating greater opportunities for higher education
access. Thus far, the undocumented immigrant students' advocacy movement has won victories in 10 states and continues to push other state
legislatures to address the question of undocumented students' access to
institutions of higher education.

The first effort to provide college access to undocumented students
culminated with the passage of an in-state tuition law in Texas in 2001.
The victory in the Texas legislature was preceded by smaller successful
battles at the community college level. Advocates, particularly in the
Houston area, used the victories at the community college to press for
changes across the state. Immigrant advocates and immigrant students
were pivotal throughout the process, waging a concerted and organized
effort in support of HB 1403, filed in the spring of 2001 by Rick Noriega
(D-Houston) and Domingo Garcia (D-Dallas). A statewide strategy to
mobilize support for the bill laid the foundation for a broad coalition
between undocumented students and immigrant advocates that included
high school teachers, labor representatives, and public officials to ensure
a successful passage of the bill.

Texas is a large and important state with a significant and historic
undocumented population, so its passage of this legislation established a
precedent that rallied supporters around the country to push for similar
legislation and sparked the passage of in-state tuition legislation in nine
other states. All 10 state laws benefit those students who completed their

secondary studies in the given states irrespective of their immigration status. As of 2009, New Mexico, Oklahoma, and Texas also permit these students to apply for state financial aid. In view of the extremely low family incomes of many such students, the denial of financial aid in other states constitutes a continued bar to access higher education. One could also argue that these policies are limited concessions benefiting only a small subset of the undocumented population. Such interpretation notwithstanding, one could add that, regardless of the limitations of these laws, they represent an extension of democratic rights. This is an important gain. These efforts at the state level have effectively counteracted the demonization of these students and have raised awareness regarding their plight. Undocumented students and their advocates have been able to galvanize support beyond immigrant communities to achieve legislative victories. The unexpected continuing gains on the immigrant rights front, while far from sufficient or irreversible, point to a deeper and broader historic support for democratic rights and equal access to education, which immigrant rights supporters must continue to draw upon.

Should relief be available for undocumented persons who are here for a better life, harming no one while pursuing the American dream? The answer is YES. They do socially necessary work and they are deeply enmeshed in American society. If they participate in the economy and civic life, they ought to be regarded as potential or future full-fledged participants as well. They must possess basic civil liberties and must be set on the road to citizenship. The morally right thing to do is to recognize their contributions and circumstances and provide them with a path toward legalization.

As a nation, we must do the right thing when it comes to undocumented immigrants. We demonize the undocumented, rather than see them for what they are: human beings who come seeking a better life and who have been manipulated by globalization, regional economies, and social structures that have operated for generations. Whereas the United States has sought to be a champion of human rights throughout the world, when it comes to undocumented youth living among us, we have forsaken this policy of humanity. Instead, we have created an immigration system that literally and figuratively criminalizes and punishes them.

The justification for criminalizing the actions of undocumented immigrants is based on a notion of preserving our borders, our sovereignty, and our resources. The action is based on our fear that undocumented persons take our jobs, they cost a lot, they commit crimes, they do not speak English, and they do not share our values. Thus, they are labeled as a problem and demonized. Once they are branded as bad for the economy or as "illegal," they are dehumanized and deemed unworthy of justice or decency. This brand of xenophobia is recycled from the worst nativist periods of the nation's history—periods that respectable people look back upon with shame.

Dehumanization allows the public to ignore the faces of undocumented immigrants. Basing our immigration reform decisions on fear rather than on sound judgment keeps us from our national commitment to justice and equality for all. We should strive to be thoughtful and treat people right; to adhere to high standards of truth, justice, humility, compassion, and forgiveness. We should not condone the callous and insensitive treatment of undocumented immigrants, but, instead, implement smart integration strategies that reflect our commitment to moral and civil principles of justice and community. We must object to the intolerance espoused by those who are narrow-minded and, instead, demand tolerance, humanity, and fairness of our political and civic leaders.

Getting Involved

In light of the relentless anti-immigrant campaigns, and to continue advancing the fight for undocumented immigrant rights, we must continue to advocate for change on the basis of principles of basic fairness and democratic rights. Now is the time for significant and meaningful reform. This requires that we extend constitutional protections on the basis of the Equal Protection clause of the Fourteenth Amendment to the undocumented, particularly youth who are seeking access to higher education.

The student narratives, along with the social, economic, and civil rights arguments, presented in this book make an undeniable case for legalization of undocumented students. Nevertheless, efforts to do so have stalled in Congress. Renewed efforts are needed to bring this issue to the forefront. Everyone can play a role by becoming involved in lobbying state and federally elected officials, supporting grassroots and lobbying organizations that work on behalf of immigrants, and educating other concerned citizens through word of mouth and encouraging them to become involved in supporting undocumented youth and their families. It should be noted that support for legislation to legalize undocumented students is not limited to immigration advocates and their supporters. Support for legalization ranges across the social and political spectrum. Table 1 provides only a partial listing of organizations and elected officials who support legalization legislation.

There are various ways to get involved. The first step is to call and e-mail your elected officials in Congress, letting them know that you want them to support legislation legalizing undocumented students. Encouraging your friends, relatives, and co-workers to do the same is another way to become an activist. To find your congressional representatives and their contact information, you can enter your address at congress.org, in the box labeled, "Find Your Officials." Another way to get involved is to donate time and/or money to grassroots and nonprofit organizations that advocate and lobby for legislation to support undocumented students. Table 2 provides a list of some of these organizations and their websites. You can also join various Facebook and MySpace groups by searching for them using the keyword, "DREAM Act."

Conclusion

If the debate continues to question whether undocumented immigrants should receive financial aid, conflicting policies will miss the critical question of who should be eligible for this benefit. This book argues that undocumented students and their families are substantive members of American society and should receive legal status. Our current immigration laws fail to recognize the multitude of ways in which undocumented students and their families contribute to the health and vitality of our social institutions and communities. Only federal legislation has the

TABLE 1
Organizations Supporting Federal Initiatives to
Legalize Undocumented Students
Official Support

American Federation of Teachers
Asian Pacific American Legal Center of Southern California
Associated Students Inc., California State University, San Marcos
California Association of Bilingual Education
California Community College Board of Governors
California Federation of Teachers AFL-CIO
California State Senator Gill Cedillo (D-Los Angeles, District 22)
California State Student Association
California Together: Education Roundtable
Community College League of California
Hispanic Association of College and Universities
"I Have a Dream" Foundation
Los Angeles Area Chamber of Commerce
Mexican American Legal Defense and Educational Fund (MALDEF)
National Education Association
National Immigration Forum
National PTA
South Bay Labor Council AFL-CIO
The National Immigration Law Center
Union of Needletrades, Industrial and Textile Employees

---

power to revise immigration law to allow these students to adjust their status and end the burden of discrimination and the dehumanizing branding of the terms *illegals* and *aliens*. The message federal, state, and local governments send, and the media echo, is that these students and their families—among the most impoverished groups who are locked in low-paying, dead-end jobs—are a threat to U.S.-born citizens. In contrast, legal incorporation of undocumented youths and their families is a question of dignity and fundamental human rights.

TABLE 2
Immigration Advocates

Organization	Website
Asian Pacific American Legal Center	http://www.apalc.org
California Immigrant Welfare Collaborative	http://www.nilc.org/ciwc/
Center for Community Change	http://www.communitychange.org/
Central American Resource Center	http://www.carecen-la.org
Coalition for Human Immigrants Rights of Los Angeles (CHIRLA)	http://www.chirla.org
Friends Committee on Legislation of California	http://www.fclca.org
Korean Resource Center	http://www.krcla.org
Legislation Information of California	http://www.leginfo.ca.gov/
Mexican American Legal Defense and Educational Fund (MALDEF)	http://www.maldef.org
NAFSA: Association of International Educators	http://www.nafsa.org/
National Council of La Raza	http://www.nclr.org
National Immigration Law Center	http://www.nilc.org
National Korean American Service & Education Consortium	http://www.nakasec.org
Salvadoran American Legal and Educational Fund	http://www.salef.org
Voces de la Frontera	http://www.vdlf.org/

Reading Group Guide

Twenty-six years ago, the Supreme Court affirmed undocumented students' right to a public education in the Plyer v. Doe (1982) decision. The decision applies to elementary and secondary schooling—thus safeguarding education only through high school. This leaves the students who aspire to further their education with very few options for achieving a college degree.

Through the inspiring stories of sixteen students—from seniors in high school to graduate students—*We ARE Americans* gives voice to the estimated 2.4 million undocumented students in the United States. These stories reveal how, despite financial hardship and the unpredictability of living with the daily threat of deportation—and often in the face of discrimination by their teachers—many of these students are not just persisting in the American educational system, but excelling. Not only do they shine academically, they are also often participating in local community service projects. This collection of narratives reveals what drives these young people and the visions they have for contributing to the country they call home.

We ARE Americans draws attention to these students' predicaments, stimulating debate about putting right a wrong not of their making, and motivating more people to call for legislation, such as the stalled DREAM Act, that would offer undocumented students who participate in the economy and civil life a path to citizenship.

Questions for Discussion

Q. The topic of immigration is without doubt very controversial in the United States. Why do you think immigration is such a charged topic? What are seen as the pros and cons of immigration?

Q. Do you feel undocumented students are a potential economic asset instead of a drain on the economy? Why or why not?

Q. Despite the actual facts about undocumented immigrants helping the economy, the stereotypes about immigrants as "lawbreakers" or "abusers of social services" seem to linger. Why do you think this happens? How do you think these stereotypes affect undocumented students?

Q. Were your perceptions of undocumented students transformed or reinforced by this book? Have your notions about what it means to be "American" changed since reading the book? What makes someone "American"?

Q. Do you feel that the undocumented students described in this book are as American as students born in this country? Why or why not?

Q. Did you identify with or have a strong emotional reaction to any of the personal narratives presented in this book? Did any of the narratives make you happy, sad, angry, or disappointed? If so, which one(s)?

Q. Lack of federal financial aid is one of the greatest barriers undocumented students face in gaining access to higher education. Why does our society and government resist rectifying this situation? Do you think there are solutions?

Q. The personal narratives in this book highlight the high levels of civic engagement undocumented students participate in during their educational careers. Do you think the contributions undocumented students make should entitle them to a path toward legalization? Why or why not?

Q. The stories of the formerly undocumented students that conclude the book show that legalization is enabling them to make a positive contribution to society and their local communities. Do you believe that legalization of such students will result in a net benefit to society?

Q. Do you think schools (K–12 & universities) should play a role in helping undocumented students achieve success? If so, what role should schools play?

Q. Are you convinced by the argument that the constitution provides basic rights and guarantees to every young adult, even if they came to this country without legal authorization? Why or why not? These principles were used in the arguments which won primary and secondary education for undocumented children. What, then, are the arguments for and against giving them citizenship? Or access to funding for higher education?

Q. Do you think the United States needs to rethink current immigration policies to be more inclusive? Does the U.S. government need to pass legislation for more comprehensive immigration reform? Why or why not?

Q. On page 91 Lucia says:

> "I wasn't asked to be brought here. I didn't choose to come here. I didn't ask for my situation. I feel like it's a punishment. I did everything I was told to do. I stayed out of trouble. I stayed out of gangs. I didn't get pregnant at sixteen. I'm a great member of society. I know more of civic duty than most naturalized or U.S.-born citizens. I know more about politics than most U.S. citizens. So why am I being punished?"

How does this make you feel, as an "American"? As a person? What would you do in Lucia's place?

Q. In many of the student narratives, individuals play an important part in either getting the student started or facilitating their further path: Lilia's teacher, page 27; Paulina's family, page 54; Lucia's teachers and employer, page 89; Jessica's counselor, page 117. What are people doing to help the undocumented students in your schools? What would you be willing to do?

Q. Perez writes that immigrants do socially important work—in fact, our economy depends on them. We cannot expect these workers—who are important links in our economic chain—not to want to be with their families. So how do we deal, as a country, with this catch 22? Would you be willing to keep out all of the workers and pay more for many goods and services? Or acknowledge the part they play and thus educate and legalize their children?

Q. On March 26, 2009 the DREAM Act was reintroduced in Congress. If passed it would allow a path to legalization for undocumented students who graduate from high school and continue on to college or to serve in the military. Do you think the stories profiled in this book would compel most Americans to contact their Congressional representatives to encourage them to vote for the DREAM Act? Why or why not? Do the stories compel you to contact your congressional representative in support of the DREAM Act?

INDEX

Also available from Stylus

Sentipensante (Sensing/Thinking) Pedagogy
Educating for Wholeness, Social Justice and Liberation
Laura I. Rendón
Foreword by Mark Nepo

"What would happen if educators eschewed the silent agreements that govern institutions and established a new set of working assumptions that honor the fullness of humanity? In this visionary study, Laura Rendón lays the groundwork for a pedagogy that bridges the gap between mind and heart to lead students and educators toward a new conception of teaching and learning. Grounding her work in interviews of scholars who are already transforming the educational landscape, Rendón invites the reader to join a burgeoning movement toward more inclusive classrooms that honor each learner's identity and support education for social justice. Her book is vital reading for anyone seeking to create more inclusive institutions for students and teachers alike."—*Diversity & Democracy (AAC&U)*

"Rendón has written a pedagogic masterpiece with immense potential to transform teaching and learning in the K–12 system. Her pedagogy gives voice to what teachers have been yearning for in their hearts and minds."—*Héctor Garza, President, National Council for Community and Education Partnerships, Washington, DC, and Monterrey, Mexico*

Ethnicity in College
Advancing Theory, and Improving Diversity Practices on Campus
Anna M. Ortiz , Silvia J. Santos

This book explores the importance, and construction, of ethnic identity among college students, and how ethnicity interfaces with students' interactions on campus, and the communities in which they live. Based on qualitative interviews with White, Latina/o, African American and Asian students, it captures both the college context and the individual experiences students have with their ethnicity, through the immediacy of the students' own voices.

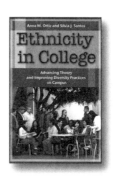

The Latina/o Pathway to the Ph.D.
Abriendo Caminos
Edited by Jeanett Castellanos, Alberta M. Gloria, Mark Kamimura
Foreword by Melba Vasquez, Hector Garza

"This edited volume fills a significant gap in the literature by serving as a resource for Latina/os who are either interested in pursuing a doctorate or who are currently in a doctoral program. Students, faculty, and administrators committed to enhancing the numbers of Latina/o Ph.D. students will consider this book a resource filled with a wealth of insight and knowledge."—*The Review of Higher Education*

22883 Quicksilver Drive
Sterling, VA 20166-2102

Subscribe to our e-mail alerts: www.Styluspub.com